Despard, the spy, or, The fall of Montreal

W. Hamilton

DESPARD, THE SPY;

OR,

THE FALL OF MONTREAL.

BY W. J. HAMILTON,

Author of the following Dime Novels

NEW YORK:

BEADLE AND COMPANY, PUBLISHERS,

98 WILLIAM STREET.

(No. 172.)

710900

DESPARD, THE SPY.

CHAPTER I.

THE SPY.

Was it a cry for help?

The night was dark as Erebus, and the city lay wrapped in its sable mantle. But, out of the gloom of the street called Nôtre Dame, came a low cry, stifled immediately after. Few persons were on the avenue, and most of these were soldiers, intent upon some duty, who passed along with hurried steps. One man, muffled in a cloak, paused as he heard the sound, and laid his hand upon his sword. The sound was not repeated, and he passed on, turning the corner toward Great St. James. As he did so, he met a party of three men, two of whom bore some burden between them, which looked like a human body. The man did not hesitate, but, drawing his sword, sprung at them, shouting, in French:

"*Halte là!*"

They paused at the summons, and lowering their burden to the pavement, the rattle of steel was heard, while a stern voice demanded:

"Who is he would stop us in the pursuit of our business?"

"One who will have an answer," replied the man in the cloak. "I heard a cry. Who is it you are bearing away between you? By heaven, the cry I heard sounded like the voice of a woman. If it should prove so, then look to yourself."

"Excuse me, monsieur. It seems to me, though perhaps I may be wrong, in which case you will of course correct me where I err, that you take an unwarrantable liberty in thus putting yourself in the way of a man engaged in the performance of a vow."

"I am not the man to interfere without warrant," replied

the gentleman in the cloak. "But, by our Lady of Mercy, you shall show me that this is not a lady you are carrying away. If it be a man, go your ways, in God's name. It is different with a woman. In that case you carry her onward only above my dead body."

"Have your way then," said the spokesman of the opposing party, in a tone of concentrated passion. "Down with this stubborn knave!"

A rush was made at the single man. It was a day when men put every thing to the arbitration of cold steel, and no people were more forward than the French, to whom fighting was and is a pastime. Yet it is no light thing to meet an attack from three swordsmen in the dark. The gentleman did no such thing. Dodging past them in the darkness, catching their thrusts in his cloak, at the risk of an awkward cut or two, he snatched up the prostrate body and dashed out of the dark street into Nôtre Dame street again. Here, near the corner, a watch-fire gleamed, and three musketeers were on duty. One of them sprung forward and advanced his weapon, with the usual challenge:

"*Qui est là!*"

"A friend, with the countersign."

"Advance, friend, and give the countersign."

The gentleman gave the word, and darted up to the fire.

"I am pursued, my lads," he said. "Let us give the fellows a reception. Here is light enough for our purpose."

The men laughed at the coolness of the speaker, and made ready their weapons as he laid his burden down.

At the same moment the pursuers came round the corner. Seeing the watch-fire and the figures of the guard, they felt that discretion was the better part of valor, and turning again, buried themselves in the darkness. The man in the cloak now looked toward the burden he had carried, and began to unwrap the long cloak in which it was swathed. As the last fold came off, and the light of the watch-fire fell full upon it, he saw the face of a lady, of all others the belle and pride of Montreal, Marie D'Arigny. She was bound hand and foot, and a gag thrust into her mouth. With a muttered curse, responded to by the "sacrés" and "scelerats" of the guard, the gentleman cut the cords and released her.

"Mademoiselle D'Arigny," said he, in the cold, even tone he had used throughout, "you know that I am not demonstrative, and you will believe me when I say that I am glad to be of service to you."

"Thanks, Monsieur Despard," replied the lady, in a low, musical voice. "You have saved me from an unknown fate, one I tremble to think upon. I shall never forget it, and he whom I love will remember it too."

"It is for his sake that I care for you," said the man called Despard, for the first time showing a touch of feeling. "But, this is not the time or place to speak of it. Are you injured?"

"Not in the least, though I was seized somewhat roughly," replied the lady.

"If mademoiselle will excuse me," said the sergeant who was with the guard at the time, "I must ask her a few questions."

"Certainly. You only do your duty. I am ready to answer," she replied.

"Thanks. Then, in the first place, how did you find yourself in such a situation?"

"Easily enough. In passing down St. James a little time ago, I was suddenly set upon by three men. I had only time to utter one cry, when I was nearly strangled."

"Does mademoiselle infer that there is a man in Montreal ruffianly enough to seize a lady by the throat?" gasped the sergeant.

"_I_ found one," was the reply.

"A Frenchman; and he knew it was a woman?"

"Without doubt. He spoke in a disguised voice, but his French was pure. There is no mistake in it."

"It is a disgrace to France," said the soldier, drawing himself up, proudly. "And yet, _can_ such a man disgrace a country like France? It can not be. If I find him, and do not give him my compliments, clothed in steel, may my right hand forget its cunning. Far better is the man known as the Silent Slayer, the Englishman who escaped from prison not long since. If he was an enemy, he was at least a brave man, and bore a heavenly blade."

Marie D'Arigny blushed. She had a reason for knowing

the young provincial of whom he spoke. Despard's grim
face relaxed into a smile.

"But, that is not to the point. Mademoiselle will have the
goodness to go on," said the sergeant.

"My hands and feet were tied, and I was lifted from the
ground and carried down the street. We were soon stopped
by Monsieur Despard, who called them to a halt. I fainted
then, for I remember nothing up to the time my friend removed the cloak from my person."

"I can tell you the rest in few words, sergeant. I met
them, snatched the lady from them, and ran. The rest you
know yourself," said Despard.

"I will know more yet before this time to-morrow night,"
said the sergeant, "or my name is not Pierre Soule. They
shall find that ruffians can not perform such feats as these under the very eyes of the muskeeters of the guard. I, for one,
will not endure it. I will see my captain and inform him."

"Who is your captain ?"

"Captain Jean Lamont."

"I know him. A worthy soldier, an honorable man.
That is the least praise I can give him. I hear he is to be
sent to Quebec in a day or two."

"So it seems."

"I shall be sorry to lose him. We have got so used to
seeing his kind face about the barriers, that it does not seem
right for him to go."

"De Levi needs him. Soldiers must not complain, monsieur, especially a soldier of France."

"Right, sergeant. But, can you give us a guard to the
residence of Mademoiselle D'Arigny ?"

"Certainly. I will go with you myself, if you please."

Despard gave Marie his arm, and the two walked away toward the cathedral, with the sergeant marching stiffly in the
rear. It was a short walk to the house, which stood in the
midst of noble grounds, and was itself a well-built mansion,
for the time.

"Will you walk in, Monsieur Despard ? I have something
to say to you."

"With pleasure."

"Before you go, Sergeant Soule," said the lady, "take this,

not as payment for your services, which can not be paid with money, but to drink my health at the Fleur de Lis."

"The soldiers of France have always money enough to buy a flagon of wine to empty in honor of a lady of quality," said the soldier. "I can not take money for such a purpose. But, if you care to give it to me for a disabled comrade, who lacks some little luxuries he might have for money, I shall be well pleased."

Marie added two more broad golden pieces to those already in her hand, and gave him the five. He looked pleased.

"Where is your comrade?" she asked.

"In the hospital, mademoiselle."

"I knew nothing of it. Will you give me his name? I will see him to-morrow."

"You, mademoiselle?"

"Why not? I see many sick soldiers. You have not given me his name."

"It is Jules Danton. If you would see him, it might cheer the boy's heart. He is a young fellow, mademoiselle— a boy to me, but I love him. To a rough old soldier such as I am, mademoiselle, such a love seems necessary. Perhaps you would not think so. Nevertheless, it is true; and I love this child."

"Then you have my promise: I will see him to-morrow."

"You have my thanks, mademoiselle. I will never forget it. Good-night."

As his retiring footsteps were heard, they turned into the house. Marie had a pass-key, with which she entered, and led the way herself to a small parlor, in which a fire was burning cheerily.

"This is my sanctum," she said, pointing to a book-case. "Here, with my guitar, my harp, and my books, I pass my happiest hours."

A few words of explanation seem necessary at this point. Marie had lost a brother not long before, who was killed on an island in Lake Champlain, by a trusted friend, Mariot Dujardin. His crime was then known to Marie, Despard, and Captain Lamont, Wilton, known as the Silent Slayer, the Indian called the Giant Chief, and an Irish friend of Wilton's. Not one of these dared expose his crime, for the reason that others would be compromised by such an act, whom it was important to shield. So it was concluded to let him run his full course of crime, and he was even now in Montreal, seeking in every way to gain the hand of Marie, the prize for which he had reddened his hand with the blood of her brother. He hated Wilton because he was beloved by Marie, but the young American had escaped from his hands.

"You are not always unhappy, as I am," said Despard, answering the last remark of Marie. "You do not sit, as I do, through the sad night, beside a desolate hearth, upon which the ashes lie, cold as the hopes of my sad heart."

She looked at him in surprise. She had always regarded him as a man devoid of feeling, save his hatred of France. For, though he lived among the French, and had been reared by a French family, he was in reality an Englishman, and hated the French with a fervor which was something wonderful. For years he had remained in Montreal, giving the English spies accurate information respecting the plans of the French, which information was of great importance to the former in carrying on their campaigns against the latter.

"You speak sadly," she said, noting that his hair was turning gray, although he could not have been more than thirty-five years of age. "I wish I could say something which would make you less so."

"You can do nothing," he answered. "Mine is an abiding sorrow, which will carry me to my grave long before the time allotted to man. I feel that I can not endure this nightly agony for many years. It was that which drove me out into the street to-night, for there I can best keep down the tumult which is going on in my heart. It is a terrible thing to sit alone forever, as I must do. A curse upon France! I hate the country; I hate its laws."

"Why, what evil has she done you?"

"Such a wrong as I can not name," said he. "Such a wrong as turns a heart naturally gay to bitterness. One day I may tell you all. But, do not speak of it now. When Wilton comes, I promise to tell my story, and leave you to judge whether I have any cause to love France. When did you last hear from Wilton?"

"From Ticonderoga."

"Had he been in the garrison?"

"I fear so."

"That young rogue will live to be hung yet," said the other, with a smile. "He has the most impudent way of going into danger of any man I ever saw. Witness him here, hail-fellow-well-met with Lamont and Dujardin, and the nephew of the Governor, drinking and fencing with them, as perfect a Frenchman as you could wish to see. I am a good Frenchman myself, but I take no merit in it, for I was brought up among them. He has picked up all he knows of French by himself."

"I have written to him to beware of thrusting himself into danger, but he is too venturesome for his own good. He says that he has his duties to perform, and he will do them bravely. I know him well enough to be sure of that. He has a noble heart."

"You are right. Of all men on earth, he is chief of the few that I can love and trust. No Frenchman can be my friend, because I hate the very name of France. Did you know that the English troops are coming down upon the island?"

"Is it true?"

"Yes. Wilton has sent me a token which only we can read. It was left at a hollow tree upon the bank of the river, near the rapids."

"Who left it?"

"A half-breed, in the pay of the English, who has a cabin on the upper Champlain. This is the sign. You can not, of course, solve the riddle."

He took three small sticks from his bosom, and spread them out upon the table which stood at his elbow. They were colored red, white, and blue.

"I will explain to you," he said, with a smile, "because I know you have been won over to the English side. These sticks mean the different English leaders. The green, the one in advance, signifies the Rangers of Seely and Putnam, to the first of whom Wilton is attached. They take the post of danger, from choice. The leaders of the English regular troops are growing wiser in their generation, and will admit that the provincials have good stuff in them."

" They ought, if they are like my '.ilton.   How brave he is, " said Marie, with a look of pride.

" He is the best swordsman I ever saw in my life, and I have passed it in a nation who live by the sword.   Don't get me to talking about him, or I shall not know when to stop. The boy has bewitched me, I think."

" Perhaps that is the trouble with me," said the girl, naively.

He smiled, and laid out the next stick, the white.

" This is Haviland ; they expect much of him.   The red stick is the best.   That shows that the whole force of British regulars are at hand, under Lords Rolla and Amherst.   These sticks, when I found them, were placed in such a way as to show me the probable line of march pursued by the English."

" Why could he not write this in so many words ?"

" Do you not see?   A letter, even though no names were used, would put the French on their guard, and enable them to lay plans to defeat the English, if the letter fell into their hands by any chance.   Suppose they found these sticks : they are nothing without the clue, which we only hold."

" I see that you are right and I wrong.   I should make a very poor scout."

" Spy, the French call it ; but it makes no difference : if caught, a long rope, a tavern sign for a gallows, a short shrift, and up goes the man who has done more to injure France than half the armies of Britain.   Ha ! ha ! ha !"

CHAPTER II.

A MAJOR'S WOOING.

THE hollow laugh, half insane in its intense bitterness, startled Marie.   She approached him, and kneeling by his side, laid her hand upon his arm.   As he felt the touch, a tear stole into his eye, as he saw the tender sympathy expressed in that upturned face.

"You feel for me," he cried. "Ah, what is it to feel again a woman's sympathy and woman's care! I have lived so long alone, since the blow which made me desolate, that I had almost forgotten what it is to feel that care. I thank you. Whatever my fate, this will be remembered, even in a dying hour."

"You are Wilton's friend," she said. "Once before this, you have aided in my escape from the hands of a bad man. I can not thank you enough. But, if a maiden's prayers can avail aught, then you have mine forever."

"Then you suspect some one?"

"Certainly. Who is there in Montreal so base that he would dare to seize me in that way, except Mariot Dujardin," she replied.

"It would have been better for us all if we had suffered Wilton to finish him that night by the river when they fought. Much sorrow would have been saved. He is an able and determined villain, but he has tied our hands. To betray him is to betray a dozen others, good men and true, who do not love France. I fear the subtle knave suspects that, for some reason, we dare not assail him. He acts like it."

"I met him in the street this morning, and his evil smile made me afraid. He never spoke a word, but he laid his hand upon his heart, and bowed low to me in mockery. He—"

At this moment came a rap at the door. Marie looked up in surprise. Who could have occasion to visit her at that hour? She went to the parlor window, from whence to look out upon the veranda. But one man was there, and him she decided to admit. Making a motion to Despard to go into a small room to the right of the fireplace, she opened the door and admitted the man who stood there—a dark-faced, handsome fellow, in the uniform of a major in the Canadian troops.

"Mariot Dujardin!" she cried, starting back. "What brings you here?"

"My inclinations, my charming mademoiselle. It has been so long since I have had the pleasure of speaking with you face to face. Excuse me for the intrusion."

While speaking, he had laid his plumed chapeau upon the

hall table, and walked into the little parlor without waiting for an invitation.

"*Gentlemen,* when visiting a lady, usually wait until they are *asked* to stay before they remove their hats," said Marie, who hated the major cordially. "Upon my honor, sir, you presume too much."

"By no means, my too-charming relative; ma belle cousine, you are wrong. It is no more than fair that a man who has been unavoidably separated from one he loves for a long period, should waive ceremony when at last they are brought together."

"I must be excused if I do not see the occasion for Captain Dujardin's visit," said the girl, "when I have forbidden his entrance to the house."

"Major Dujardin, my dear girl. Do you not see these toys upon my shoulder? I am promoted for my attempt to retake your English lover, whom may all the saints confound. Oh, if I get him once again within the length of my sword, it shall go hard but I will make him sure. A curse upon him, black-hearted villain that he is!"

"Did you come here that you might curse him, Mariot Dujardin?—for I will not give you the title earned by crime and treachery. Do you dare to insult him, who is as much above you *now* as he was on the night when he beat you down before his sword and set his foot upon you? Then, but that he shows mercy even to a snake which shows submission, you would have died the death you deserve. Did you not confess, that night, that it was you who killed my brother?"

"Yes; I grant I did," he said, coolly.

"Then why are you here? You can not hope that my heart will ever relent toward you. No, Mariot Dujardin; if I had a dagger in my hand now, I think I should have the heart to strike you dead. Beware of me!"

"You are a greater spitfire than ever; but I care not."

"Say you so? Leave me, then. The air you infect with your breath is odious to me. Your hateful face makes me shudder as I think that, with that face, covering to a tiger heart, you stabbed one to the death who had trusted you as a friend."

"Why did the fool defy me? Why did he say to me that I should never marry you? It was his own fault."

"You are speaking of my brother, the man you killed," she said, her eyes in a blaze of passion.

"A fool go with his soul, go where it will," said Dujardin. "Why did he force me to do it? The blade was in my hand before I knew it. Let him alone; he only got his due."

"Leave this house, which you have made so desolate, and never again pollute it with your tread. I hate you, as I do any snake that crawls and hisses. Do not speak to me again."

"I am not good-natured enough to agree to that. Do ask any thing in reason, Marie, and it shall be granted. Sit down here by me."

He had taken a seat upon a small sofa, and left room for her by his side.

"Leave the house!" she cried.

"Bah! Do not make me think you have so poor an opinion of my good sense. I came to talk with you. Stand, if you prefer, but answer my questions. When are we to be married?"

"Fool, as well as villain, *never!*"

"Complimentary, to be sure! But then, when one is used to these little affectionate terms, one cares little for them, and you have lavished them liberally on me. At the same time, that is not an answer to my question."

"Let this be your answer: When truth and honor are forgotten on the face of the earth—when the sun will not shine nor the moon give her light—when treason is honorable and murder a virtuous act—and when there is no longer steel, bullet or cord to end your hateful life, then I will be your wife."

"Strong—smells of sulphur. When— and so forth. I won't go over that string of affected nonsense. Imagine all you have supposed has come to pass, and get ready to be my wife; for I swear to you that, by fair means or foul—and I am not at all particular which—you shall be mine. Twice I have attempted to get possession of your person. As many times, thanks to the devil, I have failed. On the third trial

I shall succeed; so look to it.   I ask you to yield gracefully, while you can."

"I never will yield, Mariot Dujardin," she replied.   "I will perish by my own hand before I will be more to you than I am."

"You will be my wife, nevertheless."

"I am betrothed to a man who is as much above *you* as heaven is above earth—to a man who is a soldier, loyal to his country, to God, and to his love.   There is something grand in loving and being loved by such a man.   I feel ennobled every hour as I think of him.   And then, how small, how pitiful, how mean you look, compared with him!   *You*, then, are the man who insulted me to-night?"

"You were seized by my orders."

"You are bold to come here and say this to me.   Why should I not inform against you?"

"To say the truth, I can not tell.   It is sufficient for me that you dare not do it.   Whatever the reason, you do not mean to bring my confessions against me.   I imagine that your reasons are, that your witnesses are men who have done a traitorous act which the Governor would punish.   I know I am safe."

Despard was right when he called him an able and subtle villain.   The spy, in his concealment, ground his teeth in a rage.   He saw that it was impossible to make any accusation lie against this man.   To do it, the only witness would be Captain Lamont, himself, and Marie.   But, they had heard the confession while in the act of rescuing Wilton from prison. Despard shrugged his shoulders and kept quiet.

"Suppose you are right; suppose that we have reasons for not bringing you to the felon's dock," added Marie.   "At least I can appear against you for this last infamous and criminal act."

"Your witness, my dear girl.   I confess to *you*, in confidence, that I *did* attempt to abduct you to-night: that I was on the ground in person, and superintended the work.   It was a good plot, and would have succeeded if some son of darkness had not come in and snatched you from me.   I repeat, I tell you in confidence that I did it.   But, when I come to court, I will swear that you are wickedly deceived, and that

I never dreamed of such an act.   You have no witness; and so—"

"A mistake on your part, Major Dujardin," a calm voice interrupted.

Dujardin turned in a fury, grasping his sword by the hilt, and met the calm, bold eyes of Despard, who stood in the doorway of the little room, looking at him with an air of mild superiority.

"Villain!" roared the major, "how came you here?"

"I came in at the door, major.   An *invited* guest, by the way.   I see you do not wait for such little formalities as an invitation.   Bah!   What does it matter?   Impudence is better than politeness where such men as you find grace."

"You had better look to yourself, sir.   Who made you a spy upon my actions?"

"No one.   You forced yourself in against the wishes of the lady, and spoke in a key loud enough to be heard in the street.   You have this night confessed enough to hang you. I think you had better leave the house."

"I do not intend to be bullied by you, sir," said Dujardin, beginning to bluster.

"I do not seek to bully you.   I give you a small piece of advice; it is for you to judge whether it is good or not.   I think it is for your own good to go away now.   Not only did I overhear the little confession you made to Mademoiselle D'Arigny even now, but I was the fortunate individual to rescue her from your hands this evening.   I will swear to your voice, though disguised."

"You shall repent this act," roared Dujardin.

"Go!"

Despard spoke with a voice which was unmistakable.

"Did I understand you?" said Dujardin.

"Go!" repeated Despard.

"You have made an enemy to-night who will not forget you, Despard.   I have had my doubts of you for a long time, and now I am sure I am right.   Look to it.   No man ever wronged Mariot Dujardin yet who did not suffer for it."

"You have a ready hand upon a dagger-hilt," said Despard. "Of that I am aware.   You heard what I said, and force me to say it for the third time: *Go!*"

Dujardin left the room slowly, his eyes full of hate. Despard watched him keenly until the door closed behind him, and then turned the key quickly.

"I must be off, mademoiselle, and get to my house before he has time to gather his ruffians, or I shall never see another sunrise. He will let you alone while I am above-ground, however. Is there no way by which I can get out from the back of the house?"

"Yes; come with me."

She lifted a lamp to lead the way, but he took it from her.

"No lamps," he said. "They have betrayed many a man ere now. Give me your hand and lead the way."

Taking his hand, she led him through the dark passages to a door in the rear of the residence. Behind it the grounds were full of young fruit-trees and choice plants. They pursued a narrow path to a gate set into the garden wall, which she unlocked. Despard then pressed her hand, and without a word darted down a side street at his best speed, taking a course toward the eastern side of the city. For nearly a mile he hurried on in silence, keeping the center of the street, until he reached a small wooden house near the inside barrier, which defended the city. It was a small, low, antique building, with white-washed walls, such as we often see in St. Ann's and other ancient towns along the St. Lawrence. Even in the suburbs of Montreal to-day, especially in the French quarter, such buildings may be found. Despard ran to the window and rapped on the glass in a peculiar manner. The door opened almost instantly; the spy darted in, and dropped the heavy bars before the door immediately.

"What is the matter?" said a harsh voice.

The voice appeared to come from the floor. Despard looked down. A man, crippled and deformed to a degree that seemed incredible, was crouching there. If standing erect, he would have made a well-proportioned person; but, by some accident or crime, his back was so deformed that he walked with his face always looking at the floor, aided in his course by two short canes.

"I was pursued, good Conrad," said Despard, who spoke to the deformed wretch with the utmost tenderness; "but, I

think I have thrown them off the scent.   There are few men
in Montreal who know of the many places where I can hide
my head from pursuit.   Has any one been here?"

"Speak to the purpose first," replied the deformed man, in
his harsh, guttural voice.   "I must know if you are in any
danger.   If so, away; find another hiding-place.   Andrew
Despard can have no rest as long as his mission remains un-
accomplished.   How say you?   Are you in dread?"

"It is no one who has force enough to break in.   They
may come to the door.   If they do, open the wicket and
threaten them with the soldiers at the barriers."

A loud knock interrupted him as he was going on with the
speech, and a loud voice demanded admittance.   Despard
stepped into a little curtained recess apart from the large room,
and peeped out from the curtains.   The deformed man pushed
a chair up to the door, and mounting on it with an agility
which no one would have supposed him capable of, opened a
little wicket, not four inches square, and listened.

"Open here!   Open in the name of the Governor!" cried
a voice, which Despard had no difficulty in recognizing as that
of Dujardin.

"Who are you?" screamed Conrad, "that dare come here
in the night to rouse a poor deformed man from the only rest
he knows?   Conrad Dumont has enough sorrow without any
more being added."

"We have pursued a man to this place for attempting the
life of Major Dujardin," cried another voice.   "His name is
Despard.   He has been seen to enter here before, and he is
here now."

"You lie, you crop-eared villain.   Now may the curse of
the eye that never sleeps, of the hand which is palsied, and
the ear that can not hear, fall on you, and blight you, body
and bones!   May you cry for rest, even in the grave, and
never attain it!   May your food be poison and your drink the
oil of upas!   If you have children, the ban of deformity fall
on them, as it has fallen on me!   Away, you scum!   I charge
you, haunt not about my doors!   I am Conrad the sorcerer,
whom ye all fear."

"For the sake of all the saints, Major Dujardin," said the
last speaker, "come away from this.   That deformed lump

has a power such as few men possess. He is a sorcerer, and can reveal secrets which we think locked in silence."

"Major Dujardin is there," said Conrad. "I have never seen his face, but he is there. Let me give him my blessing, such as so great a villain deserves. He is a murderer. I can see the blood upon his hands, even here."

"Conrad, Conrad!" whispered Despard, "beware!"

"Down with the door and stop his cursed tongue!" cried Dujardin.

"May the marrow leave the bone and the hand be palsied that touches the door," shrieked Conrad. "Hear my blessing. The light of the withered heart fall on you, Mariot Dujardin—the curse of a heart always weary and full of bitterness. May no hope of yours ever meet its full fruition. Disappointment and sorrow follow you through life. Hope deferred make the heart sick: may your friends turn traitors in the hour when you need them. May your life be one eternal night of sorrow. Oh for a little breath to curse you, red-handed slayer of the innocent."

Dujardin stood with bowed head while this fearful malediction rained upon him. Looking up at length, he saw the malevolent face and gleaming eyes of the deformed man peering through the little opening, within a foot of his own. His first thought was to lift his hand and strike the mocking wretch to the earth. But, the malevolent look which flamed from the eyes restrained him, and his hand dropped to his side.

"What have I done to you that you should curse me?" he demanded.

"You do not know? One day it shall be given you to understand, and in that hour call upon the rocks and the mountains to cover you, and they shall not obey you. What are the pitiful griefs of others in this world compared to mine? What are their woes? The light of happiness beside the sorrows which weigh me to the earth. Away! Why do you linger on the threshold?"

"We can not go until we know whether Despard is here concealed," replied Dujardin.

"Let me see the man among you bold enough to cross this threshold. I do not think the man lives in Montreal who would do it without the permission of Conrad the sorcerer.

Aha ! is that Monsieur le Sergeant Deschappelles I see there ? Shall I tell the tale of a crime committed by the side of the river, and how ghastly the face of the murdered man looked as it floated away under the summer sky ?"

The man to whom this speech was directed uttered a low cry of surprise and fear, at which Conrad chuckled fiercely.

" I touched you there," he cried. " There is no man among you in whose coat I can not find a hole. There is Justin Lefebre, slinking behind the major. Who broke into the house on Nôtre Dame, and stole the silver tea service and the large gold watch ?"

" Monsieur !" shouted the man, in an agony of fear, " be careful of the statements you make, or you may have to prove them."

" That is easily done, Justin. But, you are not alone in this. There are five of you, thieves, liars and murderers, every man. You are the sneak of the party. The rest are the cat's-paws to pull the major's chestnuts out of the fire."

" Endurance is past," shouted Dujardin. " Down with the door !"

Not a man stirred. Naturally superstitious, they believed that the curse Conrad had invoked would surely fall upon the man who touched the door. They looked at one another in consternation.

" Are you fools and cowards as well as what the knave called you ?" said the major. " Give me the ax."

" Hold there !" said Despard, appearing suddenly at the wicket. " I am here, Major Mariot Dujardin. What can I do for you ?"

" Ah !" stammered the other. " So you are here indeed ! You will please to come out and place yourself in my charge."

" Excuse me. Call the guard at the barrier yonder. I will go with them, not with you."

" Do you suspect me ?"

" Most decidedly. You are not the sort of company I care for in a dark night and in a narrow street. The guard at the barrier are honorable soldiers, not in your pay. It will be a pleasure to me to make a statement to the officer in charge in reference to his companion in arms, Major Dujardin."

"You are a villain."

"You certainly are, Major Dujardin," replied Despard, coolly. "Now do not think to bluster me out of my determination, or change my purpose. Either call the guard and give me in charge, or leave this place at once; for, I give you my honor, the first man who puts foot upon that door-sill, I will kill."

"You will not dare to resist?"

"I always dare to defend myself. If you think me a coward, strike but once at that door, and then look to yourself," rejoined the spy.

There was a muttering among the villains assembled about the door. They did not like the posture of affairs. This man showed too determined a front. If he had yielded to their escort, he would have gone out, never more to look upon the light of day. They would have killed him, and left his body in the street. But, the keen-witted man read them easily, and he knew that they would never call the guard, as such a course must lead to the inquiry as to what the major was doing in the street at that late hour.

"I ask you once more to give yourself up to me," said the major.

"And I once more refuse."

"Then I shall be forced to lay my claim before the Governor and council."

"Do so; I shall be charmed. My worthy major, you have not caught the fox."

The baffled villains retreated. Despard opened the door and peered out after them. There was no mistake about it. They were gone.

CHAPTER III.

WILTON.

"THE plot thickens," said Despard, closing and barring the door and dropping upon a stool near the fire. "That villain will complicate all from this hour. My curse upon him! Why should he enter the fight before his time?"

"Andrew," said the deformed one, who had crouched at the side of the fire, close to the feet of the other, "the work is before us; shall we not do it? All the devotion of my life is yours. If by doing it I could be of service to you, how gladly would I lay down this wasted being. But, I believe that even I, cramped and deformed though I am, can still be a sad sort of comfort to you."

"In more ways than one, my poor Conrad. You stir me up to the work I have to do; and if sometimes I grow weary on the road, and stop to look at household hearths on which the fires are glowing, such a hearth as was to be mine, a look at your face quickly makes me forget all but vengeance."

"True heart and bold! Bear up and be strong, even for her sake, who has passed into the valley of the shadow," said Conrad.

"For her sake! Ah, now you have named her, I am a man again, ready to do a man's work in the cause I have undertaken. I need not fear this man. He is a villain, and an acute one. We shall be more than his match, my Conrad."

"He shall see."

"How the knaves stared, when you laid their lives open before them! They little know Andrew Despard. No wonder they were appalled, for how could you, of all men, get this knowledge by fair means? It is a good plan to keep up the idea of sorcery on your part. It will be a protection to you."

"It has been, before now. There are few men hardy enough to lay the weight of a finger on me in anger. They ____ ha, ha! They think my curses will come home to ____ __e day or another. I believe it too. Who of all men

who have incurred our hatred, did not some day have cause
to feel that we have power, such as few men have? Let them
beware of Conrad! He will make their lives bitter to them."

"The work is before us, Conrad. It is a hard labor. The
French begin to suspect me, and but that I know the nets of
the English are drawing close about this doomed city, I
should fear to remain here longer. The Governor's private
Secretary looked closely at me, and whispered to the Governor
when they passed me yesterday. I begin to fear that some
one of those who have been so long in our power are kick-
ing over the traces. If the worst comes, Andrew Despard
must go, and another take his place."

The man at his feet smiled. He alone knew the wonderful resources of this spy, and how he had power to change
his looks so completely that the very mother who bore him
would not have known her son.

"The trouble is with you, Conrad. You can not change,
and if I go away, you may suffer ins t and abuse. I fear
it."

"I do not. They dare not touch me. Go about your
work, and trust to me to take care of myself. I can do it.
You have not sufficient confidence in me, Andrew. Remember that I loved her, too, as such a being can love any one
good and beautiful who was kind to him. Sometimes, in my
sad nights, I think of her as I knew her, with her brown hair
dropping about her face. Her voice was soft and low, and
when she touched me, I felt that even I had something to
live for."

"Silence, Conrad," gasped Despard. "Is it not enough
that I have lost her, but I must be made to feel it every hour
by you? My burden is hard enough to bear, heaven knows,
without any thing more being added to it. No, Conrad, I am
wrong. I see by your face that I have said too much. But,
you know how to bear with a heart so wrung as mine has
been this many a weary year."

"Do I not, Andrew? Nothing you can say will move me
to any thing but sorrow. We bear this grief together."

"Thank you. But I must go, Conrad. I have work to
do to-morrow which Andrew Despard could not appear in.
I think he had better keep quiet for a day or two."

Rap—rap—rap! Despard paused and listened. The rapping was repeated. One rap, then an interval, and two quick raps following, immediately followed by two rasping scratches at the door.

"Ha! Do you hear that, Conrad? As I hope to be saved, it is Wilton!"

He darted to the door and opened it. A slight young man, dressed in the garb of a French hunter, entered the room, and Despard dropped the bar behind him.

"You here, Wilton? You will dare more than any man I know. Do you not understand that your life is doubly forfeited now, since your escape?"

"I know it, my good Despard. But, what can you ask? One can not always control his motions; and, by the hopes of my life, I would have come to Montreal to-day though Satan himself stood at the gate. Good Conrad, how do you feel to-night?"

"I am very well," said Conrad. "I hope you are the same."

"Never better, Conrad. I should not have come to Montreal except I were in good trim. How goes the world with you? And, Despard, how is Marie?"

It was Wilton, the Yankee lover of Marie D'Arigny, who had entered the city at the peril of his life. On a previous occasion he had been captured by the treachery of Mariot Dujardin, but had escaped. If he fell into the hands of the French now, there was no hope for him. He knew this well, and took his chances, as a brave man might.

Despard received him warmly. The gallant young American had touched his hardening heart. Wilton was literally fearless, and plunged into danger as some men go into a revel. There was something wonderfully attractive in his bold, open face, as he held Despard by both hands.

"Marie," replied Despard. "She is well. I saw her to-night, and again snatched her from the clutches of that double-dyed villain, Mariot Dujardin."

"Do you tell me that?" cried the young man. "Then I have to thank you for a new favor, Despard. Upon my soul it vexes me to the heart because I let that villain go alive when I had him down."

"I have often said it. But why are you here?"

"Why? Can you ask me the question? I came in part to do my country service, and as much to see my darling Marie. It is a hard thing, Andrew Despard, to be separated so long from one we love, and to know that it brings danger to her as well as to us to visit her. But for the latter, I should have seen her more frequently. Life is nothing without love."

"So young, so brave, so reckless. This is the mirror of my own life," moaned Despard, covering his face with his hands. "Alas, Wilton, you have never heard the story of my life. You shall hear it to-night. Come with me."

They opened a little door in the rear of the house and stepped out into the gloom. It was now verging toward morning, and the hour was the darkest of the whole night. This was nothing to these men, who had threaded the streets of Montreal in darkness too often to be deceived.

They had not far to go without an adventure. Walking at a swift pace, they were suddenly halted by the barrel of a musket, laid horizontally, while a harsh voice cried out the conventional challenge.

Despard gave the word.

"The word is correct, gentlemen; but, doubtless, you have not heard the late order of the Governor. No man shall traverse the streets after the hour of ten in the evening without a pass from some person in authority."

"That is something new, it would seem," said Despard, seeking to gain time. "The word ought to be enough."

"Perhaps. But you must bear it in mind that I am not here to give orders, but to obey them. Therefore, messieurs, you will consider yourselves detained, and come with me to the officer of the guard."

"Who is he?"

"Captain Dujardin."

"The devil," muttered Wilton. "What must we do, Andrew?"

Despard admonished him to be silent by a touch upon the shoulder.

"My lad," he said, addressing the soldier, "we have no pass, except our names. If you will come nearer, I will impart them, when I think you will allow us to pass. If not, we are willing to go with you."

Of course nothing was so foreign from the intentions of the two men as to go into the presence of Dujardin. The soldier inclined his head to hear the name, and Despard bent forward to give it. There was a dull sound, as of an ax falling on a wet log, and the soldier dropped to the earth, stunned by a tremendous blow under the ear. Without waiting to see the effect of the blow, Despard seized the hand of Wilton, sprung over the fallen man, and disappeared from sight. The soldier rose slowly to a sitting posture a moment after, rubbing, with a thoughtful air, a huge lump which was rising behind the left ear. He made no attempt to rise or make an alarm, for he was a prudent person, and saw no reason why he should bring his sagacity into question by betraying the fact that he had been so overreached. So he rose to his feet, pondering slowly upon the probable force of the blow which laid him in the dust.

Meanwhile the two men hurried forward through the street. After going several blocks they paused to listen for pursuing feet, but heard none, and settled down into a swift walk.

"A good blow that, Andrew," said the young American. "By my soul, I had no intention of attending a levée held by that excellent person in office, Marlot Dujardin."

"Nor I. That soldier must be gathering himself up by this time. How he must have been astonished. I strike a heavy blow."

"I should think so. Where do we go now?"

"You wish to see Marie, I suppose?"

"By all means. How can it be done?"

"Readily enough. Enter here with me."

He opened a small gate next to the residence of Marie D'Arigny, and signed to his companion to enter.

"You have made a mistake," the young American said; "this is not the house."

"No words. I know what I am doing. Pass in," replied Despard, almost sternly.

Wilton had known him too long to say a word more. He passed in. The house before which they stood was a stone building of medium size, with tasteful grounds about it, which

seemed to be rather neglected just at present. To his surprise, Despard went to the door, and producing a pass-key
from the folds of his coat, opened the door and entered the
hall. As they did so a door swung wide on the left of the
hall, and an old woman came out. She looked surprised, and
was about to say something, when Despard checked her by a
movement of his hand.

"Where is your master, Annette?" he said.

"He is in the house," she replied, with a smile.

"I will go to him," he said. "Show this gentleman into
the parlor and have a fire lighted. Excuse me for a moment,
Wilton."

He ran up the stairs which led from the hall to the rooms
above. Wilton followed Annette into the parlor, which was
plainly but neatly furnished. She rung a bell, and a negro
appeared, who soon kindled a fire, for all the materials were
in the grate. This done, the two servants left him, and he
took a seat before the blazing wood, looking dreamily into it.
As he sat there, he was not aware that he was not alone, but
the door had opened noiselessly, and a stranger had come into
the room. It was an old man, with hair white as snow, and
a beard which dropped upon his breast, and who supported
his steps by the aid of a stout cane, the body of which was
painted to resemble the rattlesnake, while the head and neck
was thrown into a coil. The rattle, which was of iron, was
also quaintly carved into the resemblance of a real rattle.
The robe, which was thrown loosely over the person, and
gathered at the waist by a girdle, was of some soft, white
cloth. His feet were shod with sandals, which accounted
for the noiseless manner in which he had entered the room.

The young man looked up in surprise, and sprung to his
feet. But the other made a gesture which disarmed him of
all fear.

"Must I introduce myself?" asked Wilton.

"I already know that you are Wilton, better known as the
Silent Slayer, a spy of the English."

"Then Despard has betrayed me!" said the young man,
jocosely.

"He has. But need you lose faith in him? Has he not
been true to the English all these years?" said the old man.

"True as steel. If he has told you who I am it is for some good end. Tell me who you are."

"I am one who is, and who is not—a phantom, a shadow—now here, now there. It is easier to trace the course of a comet than mine. It would do you no good if I told you, yet, since you must have a name to address me by, call me Anselmo."

"Monsieur—" began the young man.

"I said not that. Address me in English. I can speak it well, and this French hangs heavy on my tongue. I am no Frenchman. If I love any man, I love Despard. He wishes you treated kindly, and it shall be done."

"More than this. I wish to see Marie D'Arigny."

"My fair neighbor. Very well. We will see what can be done. I have some faith in my ability to bring the maiden here. A good and true maid, I believe."

"Let me see the man who dare say otherwise," said Wilton, fiercely, "and he shall cross swords with me."

"Tut, tut. You are marvelously hot-headed, my dear sir. Nobody shall challenge the purity of your lady. You shall see her, if it is in my power. But, you must be hungry after your tramp from Chambly. Let us see if we can do any thing for you."

He rung a bell and a negro appeared, bearing a tray containing venison steaks, some fine wheat bread, and a flask of wine, with glasses. These he set before Wilton, on a little table, and immediately withdrew.

"Make no ceremony," said the old man, "and have no fear of Anselmo. He has nothing but kindness for you in his heart."

"Thanks," said Wilton. "You shall find that I will punish your food dreadfully. I am rather sharp-set after my tramp from the Chambly."

"Did you see any Indians by the way?"

"I passed within sight of several camp-fires, but I only saw one Indian, whom I know. I stepped into the bushes, to let him pass. It was Wenona, the Giant Chief of St. Regis."

"Listen to me, young sir. There is no nobler heart than that which beats in the broad bosom of Wenona, in all this fair land. He has in him a lofty courage, a generous spirit toward a weak enemy, and a hatred of wrong worthy the Knights of the Round Table."

"I can well believe it," said Wilton. "His strong arm rent my prison-bars, and set me at liberty, when I was in fear of my life, and should perhaps have lost it but for his help. He stood by my side one night when we rescued Marie from the hands of ruffians who had seized her. He conducted me to the shore of the lake, through bands of hostile savages. A shout from him would have brought down upon my head the weapons of a score of painted savages. You can say nothing in Wenona's praise in which I will not heartily concur."

"Let us drink his health," said the old man, taking up the flask and filling two glasses. "Let him have a bumper."

They emptied their glasses in honor of the chief, while Wilton looked closely at the old man. Where had he seen him before? There was nothing in his face which was familiar; but something in his attitude and form, which he could not understand, reminded him of some one he had known—whom, he could not tell.

"Where is Despard, sir?" said Wilton. "Is he coming down?"

"He promised that you should see your lady-love, you say?" said Anselmo.

"Yes."

"He is about that business now," said the old man. "Be not impatient."

"You forget how long it is since I have been in Montreal. After long absence from his lady, until he has seen her face a lover is always impatient."

"Good lack, that time is past with me. I am old, young man, I am old."

"Yet your eyes have in them something of the fire of youth yet."

"Perhaps. But mine has been a weary life for all that— a life full of plots and inventions—of struggling for something unattainable—of waiting and watching for something which never comes. Young man, yours is a life of danger; you go about in hourly peril of your life; but, you have yet something to sustain you, since you have not to refuse yourself the happiness of woman's companionship, the bliss of woman's love."

"Your marble has been warmed, then?" said Wilton. "You remember your love affairs to this day."

"Remember them! As if I could forget. Fill your glass again, and drink in silence. The toast is to the memory of one who has long since passed away from earth. Sorrow bore heavy upon her beautiful head, and she died. This to her memory, for I held her very dear."

They drank in silence, and the old man laid his head upon the table before him and said not a word for some moments. Wilton remained mute. Presently Anselmo raised his head, and there was nothing in his stern old face to show that a storm of passion had passed over him, leaving his heart full of bitterness.

"That is past," he said. "All have their hours of sorrow. I have mine *always*. Since I can not be happy myself, I will do what I can for others. My dear sir, if you will wait a moment, you shall see your lady."

"Quickly, then ; I am in suspense."

The old man went out. Fifteen minutes passed, and the young man was beginning to think Marie was not coming, when the door was thrown open and he had her in his arms, close up to his beating heart.

CHAPTER IV.

DESPARD'S STORY.

LOVERS have much to say when they meet after long partings. There are mutual vows to interchange, mutual griefs to bear. They tell over word by word their thoughts since last they met. Lips meet in a long kiss, and seem loth to part. There are moments in this life worth all our life before or after—moments to remember when our hair is growing gray.

He held her off from him and looked into her glowing face, so full of love for him, and then again drew her to his heart.

"My darling!" he said, "the hours have been years since we parted."

"I am glad to meet you," she sobbed; "so glad to meet you, and yet I shudder at the danger before you."

"Never mind that, dear. Think only that we have met again."

"I never was so happy. Annette came to my window just now and gave me a note from her master. It had only these words: 'Wilton is here. Come to my house. Anselmo.' You see I did not hesitate."

"Who is Anselmo?"

"A strange recluse. It is very seldom he is seen about the house. The servants will not speak about him. Annette, who often comes to sit with my housekeeper, tells her nothing. But he is a friend to me. Who brought you here?"

"Despard."

"Where is he?"

"I can not tell. He went up-stairs and sent Anselmo to me, and I have not seen him since. Anselmo said that he was making preparations for securing an interview with you."

"He is a strange man. Wonderfully reticent in his manner, brave as a lion, and full of subtle plots and contrivances. But for him, I should now be in the hands of Mariot Dujardin."

"I shall yet be even with that guilty wretch," said Wilton. "My curse upon him; can he not let you rest now? Is it not enough that he laid your brother in the grave and that we have not the power to punish him, but he must intrude upon you, and seek by every despicable means to compass his designs?"

"He is indeed a villain. I gave him that distinction long ago and he may keep it. I have no fear of him when you are by. I can not always be exposed to him."

"Nor can I be with you always, though it is my hope to remain beside you now, until my friends break through the barriers of Montreal and make the city theirs. In that good time, my sweet one, I shall make you mine, and place it out of the power of Dujardin to take you from me. Shall this be so?"

She hid her face upon his shoulder with a happy blush. A voice said:

"God bless you both, my children."

They looked up. Anselmo had entered the room, and stood with hands uplifted, as if in benediction. Both bowed their knees before him. He laid a hand upon each young head and repeated his blessing.

"My children," he said, "you have sought to know the story of Despard. "You would know why he, who is yet young, is a recluse and hermit, except so far as he must be in companionship with men to work his designs against the French, whom he hates with a deadly and enduring hatred. Your wish shall be granted. I am commissioned to tell the tale to you, two of the few upon this earth whom Despard loves. And why does he love you? Because you are of the few who trust in him and whom he trusts, and who do not betray his confidence.

"Before I begin the tale sit down by me. Not on the same side. If you do that, I fear you will not give proper attention to the story—a sad one in my eyes. Perhaps I think so, because this man Despard and I have slept in the same blanket and under the same roof for many years."

The young couple sat down, one on each side of him, and drew up to the fire, which shone upon the venerable face of the old man. Marie noted what a strong face it was. How clear-cut the outlines, and what a fire yet showed itself in his eyes.

"Andrew Despard is an Englishman," he began; "but he was born in France, and reared by French people. This accounts for his control of the French tongue. Wilton's French is only second to his, as his sword-play is far in advance. Bah! one, two! and daylight shows through the body of your opponent."

"Excuse me," said Wilton; "but, how came you to know any thing about my sword-play?"

"Perhaps Despard told me."

"He might, indeed," said Wilton; "pray go on."

"First rise and close that shutter, Wilton."

The young man rose to obey, threw open the window and put out his arm to draw in the shutter. As he did so his eyes encountered those of a man who was lounging down the street in the early morning. The man gave a start of surprise and quickened his pace. Wilton closed the shutter and returned thoughtfully to the fire. He did not half like the manner of the fellow. Besides, there was something in his face which seemed familiar. But, if mischief had been done, he could not help it, and so sat down again to listen to the story.

"I told you that Andrew Despard was born in France. The people with whom he lived and by whom he was educated, loved him. His parents were persons of distinction, exiled from their native country for some political offense, but who had taken much wealth with them to France. The old man with whom he lived, Simon St. Ongé, was a friend of his father. The older Despard died two years after he came to France and left his wife and child to the care of his old friend. The lady, who had loved her husband dearly, soon followed him to the grave, and Andrew was left in the chateau de St. Ongé.

"He was a generous youth in those days. His worst enemies would not have denied him that. As he grew up, he became a proficient in the sword-exercise and in every manly art. Few of the youth of Normandy cared to cross weapons with him. He went to college, where he distinguished himself so much, that old St. Ongé loved him more and more. It was during his vacation that he met his fate. He loved the daughter of a neighboring gentleman. I do not intend to follow the whole course of that love affair. She was beautiful. He loved her as only such natures can love, and she returned his passion. They were very happy. The time of his vacation passed in idle dalliance, in walks and talks under the sheltering groves of Normandy until he must return to Heidelberg. His term passed and he came back. A serpent had crept into the bosom of the St. Ongé family. He found vague tales to his discredit were being sown broadcast through the section. He traced them to a young man of his

own age, who had come up to Paris, in a detachment of regular troops—an ensign, just from school. His name was
Mariot Dujardin."

"Mariot!" cried Marie, in a tone of astonishment.

"The same. He was no less a villain at that time than at
the present, and these tales he set in circulation—of duels
fought at college, of young men killed, of wild orgies in the
streets and in the beer-shops, of awkward love-affairs and the
like—had been ably concocted. His insidious stories had
found their way to the ears of Terese D'Arcy. She had a
gentle, confiding nature; she had to believe the apparently
well-authenticated reports, and they cut her to the heart. He
saw her droop like a crushed flower. It was for her love
that the scoundrel invented these falsehoods. The affair came
to a head soon.

"It was at a supper, given by the officers of the garrison,
at which Andrew was present. After the wine came on, Dujardin entered, flushed and excited. He evidently had been
drinking deeply, yet his first act was to fill a goblet to the brim
and drink it to the very dregs. The toasts went round, and at
last they came to him."

The eyes of the old man were flashing with a brilliancy
which was startling.

"Were you present?" asked Wilton.

"I was," replied Anselmo, with an odd kind of smile.
"They called on Dujardin for a toast. Bear in mind that
Terese had avoided Andrew for several days, and that he was
half-mad with passion. Dujardin rose, and lifting his brim-
ming glass above his head, cried out, 'Attention!' Every one
looked at him. 'I am about to propose the health of the
Flower of Normandy, gentlemen, and I ask you to do her
justice in your glasses—my betrothed, Terese D'Arcy!'

"He needed no more than that. In an instant young Despard had leaped across the table and had him by the throat
with one hand, while he struck him in the face with the other.
'Liar! lâche!' cried he; 'I will cram the falsehood down
your vile throat!'

"The affair marched rapidly after that. Their friends drag-
ged them asunder. Neither would hear of any thing else, so
the table was cleared away, the seconds chosen and a circle

formed. In the center, stripped to the shirt and in silk stock-ings, stood the two young men. The seconds gave the word, and they closed. My heart warms now at the thought.

"It was an even match for a while, for Despard was angry, and he got a wound in the arm first. That cooled him, and he fought more warily. In ten minutes the ensign lay upon his back on that ensanguined floor, with a deep wound in his breast.

"Of course the villain made use of that. He claimed to have been set upon when in drink and forced into a combat. Despard could not deny it, and he found his reputation grow-ing worse and worse. More and more tales to his discredit got about, even while the fellow was in bed from the effect of his wound. When he was up and around again they grew worse.

"At last a murder was committed. A young man who had been loudest in talking against Andrew, and who was thought to be a tool of Dujardin, was found dead upon the highway, with a sword-thrust through the heart. Close to the body lay a handsomely-mounted pistol, with the name of Andrew Despard engraved upon the silver plate on the butt.

"They tried him for the murder, which was done upon the verge of the D'Arcy estate. He could not deny that he was in the woods at the time, for he was there, trying to get a chance to speak with Terese. While there, he heard a cry for help, and ran out; but he could see no one. The pistol was his. He had lost it from his holster the day before.

"He was sentenced to be beheaded for that crime which he never did. They remanded him to prison to await his execu-tion. He escaped and took ship for this country. Terese went mad, they said, and died. At least, he never saw her face again."

"And who is the deformed man they call Conrad?"

"A servant of Terese, one who loved her as a faithful dog loves his master or mistress, and who followed him over the sea to share his fortunes, and be revenged on Mariot Dujardin."

"I am sorry to hear this tale," said Marie, softly. "It makes me sad. Yet he is wrong to hate all France for this."

"The country whose laws condemned him, unjustly, murdered Terese D'Arcy."

"Is Despard his real name?"

"No. When you can bring that dead woman to life, then shall you know his true name."

At this moment came a heavy blow upon the door.

CHAPTER V.

WHERE IS HE?

ALL started to their feet in surprise. Wilton's first act was to draw the sword which had stood him in good stead in many a fray, and would not fail him now. Anselmo's old eye flashed fire, and he ran to the door, upon which heavy blows were falling. It was evident that the assailants, whoever they might be, did not propose to give them much time.

"Who attacks my house?" cried the old man, angrily. "I will impeach the justice of this province if I do not get full reparation for this insult."

"Open the door, then, you old curmudgeon," howled a fierce voice. "By the life of my body, I think you no better than a sorcerer. And when you dare to give shelter to an English spy beneath your roof, you lose all right to protection."

"An English spy!"

"Yes. We know that you conceal here the young American, known as the Silent Slayer. We want him. If you do not open the door, we have axes and will force it in."

"If there is no such man here?"

"You lie, old man," cried a shrill voice. "I saw him at the window."

"Suppose there are none but women in the house? My neighbor, Mademoiselle D'Arigby, is here, and my servants," replied Anselmo.

"It makes no difference," replied the first speaker, who was

Dujardin. "We will make the search. My sergeant, Langlier, swears he saw this fellow at the window."

While they were parleying, Anselmo had pulled a bell and Annette came hurrying in. "Take Monsieur Wilton to the place you know of," he said. "Leave him there and return to your room. When all is safe, ring the bell."

All this was done in a moment, but Captain Dujardin was getting impatient nevertheless. "Open the door, I charge you. Once before this night I dared not break in because I had no warrant. I have one now. Axes!"

At this time a bell rung in another part of the house. Anselmo gave a gesture of pleasure. "If you have a warrant, monsieur, far be it from me, a loyal subject of France, to refuse to open my doors at any hour. Enter."

He threw open the door with his own hands, and a dozen musketeers of the guard poured into the little hall. At the sight of Anselmo, standing before them in his white robe, they felt a sudden thrill of awe, and would have fallen back, had not their leader spoken.

"What is your name?"

"Anselmo Girard."

"Your occupation?"

"A student."

"Are you loyal to France?"

"My heart has been proved in that long ago. Has yours, Mariot Dujardin?"

"You know me, then?"

"There are few things I can not tell you in your past life, if you would have me do it, Mariot. I would take you back to the sheltering groves of Normandy. I would speak to you in the voice of a woman, long since in the silent grave, whom men called Terese D'Arcy."

"Off!" cried Dujardin, clutching at his throat as if in a fit. "Are you man or demon? What do you know of those forgotten days?"

"I know enough and more than enough, Mariot. I could speak of a duel by the mess-table, of the murder on the road, near the great grove on the D'Arcy estate. I can say more, if you like."

"Silence, madman. The air is full of sorcery to-night.

Twice already I have been reminded of those who are in their graves, and of events which before now have been covered by the dust of years. Who are you?"

"Seek not to know."

"But I will know, old dotard," cried Dujardin, grasping him suddenly by the throat. "I will understand how it is you know of events which by right are secret from you."

Anselmo shook him off with a quick movement, as if he had been a child, and darting to a bracket in the hall, took down a sword which hung there, and threw himself upon his guard, with the ease and skill of a practiced swordsman. "Come on," he cried. "You have laid your hand upon my throat. I will teach you that I have not forgotten how to meet an insult, old as I am."

But Dujardin's mood had changed. He stood in an attitude of deep abstraction, gnawing his lips and tapping his sword-hilt nervously. "Come on," repeated the old man, "unless you are a coward."

"Peace, old man," said the captain. "If I chose to notice your talk it would not be well for you."

"I fear you not," replied Anselmo.

"Doubtless. Men, to your duty. Search every nook and cranny in this old rookery. Have you placed guards outside, sergeant?"

"Yes, sir," said Langlier, saluting.

"Very good. Then forward at once. Leave no place unsearched. If he has escaped, I would give my commission to bring him back. You are sure you saw him?"

"Certain, Monsieur le Capitaine."

"How did you know him?"

"I fought him once. But I could do nothing with him. He bears a gallant sword, and I could almost forgive his conquest of me, for having crossed swords with such a man."

"I met him too, and I bear him no good will," said Dujardin. "Do your duty; and hark you, Langlier. He may resist. If he does, remember that I shall be quite as well pleased to receive his *dead* as his *living* body."

"I understand," said Langlier. "It shall go hard if you do not receive him dead. Ten Louis?"

"You shall have them."

The men by this time had gone forward and were searching the house in every direction. Anselmo, still holding his sword, had followed them. Langlier left the major standing in the hall and followed the men. Dujardin, without looking at Anselmo, turned into the little parlor. As he saw Marie standing there he came forward, with extended hands.

"My dear girl, I am glad to meet you," he said.

"I hope the time may never come when I can say the same of you, Marlot Dujardin."

"Still cruel? I had hoped that you would change."

"When you change your nature," she said. "You come here in pursuit of one I love best of any one on earth, and you expect me to look upon you kindly."

"Then he is here?" he cried, eagerly. "Else, how did you know of whom I am in pursuit?"

"You spoke loudly enough to be heard in the next street. It is no wonder that I know the object of your coming, since I have been standing here all the time."

"Then you have heard all that gray-headed fool said to me," he stammered.

"No fool, it seems to me. He gave you a good history of your past life."

"My life, mine?"

"Yes: your Normandy experiences. It seems to me that I remember something of this. It was when we were in Paris. My brother was there, you remember. When I think of him, it seems to me it would be no crime to drive a dagger into your heart. If I remember rightly, St. Julian was very hard upon you for your work in Normandy."

"Be silent; I will hear no more."

"I never thought you so old. That was ten years ago. Ten years? Quite an age, it seems to me. You must be very old."

"Some one has belied me. Hark!"

There was great confusion in the upper rooms. Dujardin flung open the door and hastened up the stairs. The noise came from a room to the left, the door of which was open. He darted in. A ring of soldiers had formed about the walls of the room, and there, fighting desperately, stood Langlier and Anselmo. The old man, in his white robe, with one foot slightly advanced, met his assailant's fierce rushes with a calm smile of derision, and parried his best thrusts with an ease and grace which astonished Langlier, who was himself an adept in the use of the weapon.

Just as Dujardin entered, the old man made a disengagement, and ran his adversary through the shoulder. He dropped his sword with a groan. Two or three of the others started forward with drawn blades, when the voice of the major recalled them.

"What is this? Answer me, Deschappelles; answer me, Langlier. I sent you to search for an English spy, and I find you engaged in a personal combat with an old man, who, I thank heaven, has worsted you."

"He may be old," growled Langlier. "Be that as it may, you could not stand before his blade."

"Nonsense; that is not an answer to my question. Why do I find you squabbling here?"

"I said something to an old woman who was in the room, and he resented it."

"He insulted a faithful servant," said Anselmo, "and if you had not come I would have carved him like a capon. I hate such rascals as he is, who pimp for some greater knave. He is the man to do murder for hire. You have chosen a fine instrument, Captain Dujardin."

"Major, you mean."

"Major! A thousand pardons. Judas got thirty pieces of silver, and when he had them, he was sorry for it. You get the price, and are pleased. Complimentary to Judas; the reverse to you."

"Disperse!" cried the officer. "To the duty I assigned you, Deschappelles! Pry into every place. I am satisfied that the Englishman is in the house."

The work recommenced. They went from cellar to garret in an unavailing search.

Wherever they went, Anselmo followed them, with the bloody sword yet in his hand, eager to take up any insult offered, and fight upon that ground. The bellicose attitude of the old man rather amused the greater portion of the guards, who Frenchman-like, respected bravery wherever they saw it.

"Where have you secreted this spy?" demanded Dujardin, as they came again to the first floor. "I desire to know."

"If yonder villain has lied to you, how am I to blame?" said Anselmo.

"He has not lied."

"Then find the man you want. As for me, I know nothing about him. If I knew I would not tell you."

"I believe that is false. Langlier is not a man to be mistaken. He says that the man who closed the blind was not three feet away, and he had a full view of his face. Upon my honor I think you are deceiving me."

"Think as you choose. I have said all I purpose to say. If you believe me, well. If not, it is not my fault, I am sure. I will go into the parlor to attend to my guest."

Dujardin followed him in. As he did so, his eye fell upon the little table whereon the wine was still standing. He snatched the bottle quickly and looked at the brand.

"Mademoiselle must be a hard drinker if she helped you to punish this bottle," he said. "Who was your companion over your wine?"

"A neighbor, who has been gone an hour. The wine has not been removed. I will call the servant and have it taken away."

"Excuse me if I taste your vintage first," said Dujardin, seating himself at the table and pouring out a glass of the wine. "Let me fill for you, ma belle cousine. Will you give me a sentiment?"

"If you like."

He handed the glass to her with a bow and a smile. She took it, and raising it high above her head, gave the toast: "Captain Dujardin; (for, as I told you, I will never give you the title earned by your treachery)—may he soon get his deserts."

"I need not ask you what my deserts may be," he said, smiling.

"I will tell you, gratis. A halter, sir; a halter."

Dujardin dashed his glass upon the floor, and rose.

"It is well for you that it is bright daylight, mademoiselle, or I would take you where you would never see daylight again, except at my command."

"I do not fear you, by day or by night," she answered, firmly.

"As for you, my worthy sir, you, who know so much of my affairs, I will yet find a day to look into yours. For the present I leave you; but, be it understood, I do not leave you without a guard. Three of my men will remain in the house, and if your worthy friend the spy returns, he does so at his peril."

"I will not have your fellows in my house."

"I do not see how you will help yourself. As for my men, treat them well and you will be treated in like manner."

"You are considerate. I will see the Governor to-day, and understand if I am to be overrun by his soldiery, because some fool chooses to think he saw a man in my window."

"You are at liberty to go to the Governor if you like. The guard you shall have."

"They will not stay here long. You shall see whether I have friends."

"I care not. I bid you good-day, mademoiselle. The time is not far distant when I shall humble your pride as low in the dust as you would have mine. See to it! The hour will come speedily."

He went away, leaving the man called Deschappelles and two others in the house. Anselmo gave them a room, but they paraded the house where they chose, at unseasonable hours. Anselmo was ill at ease. Whatever he had done with Wilton, he was in the house, and there was no way to get him out till the soldiers were removed.

"What shall we do?" said Marie. "Where is he?"

"Safe enough for the present," said Anselmo; "but so safe that there he must remain until these soldiers are gone; and he is so headstrong that I fear he will try to break out if kept there long."

"Have you a key to the place where he is?" she asked.

"It needs no key."

"Show me the place. I will engage that he will stay there if I hold the clue."

"You would starve him sooner than let him out. You can not know the place. I will attend to him and do my best."

"Am I not to see him again?"

"I can not tell. If there is danger in it, you will see him no more until the affair is over. A woman? Bah! A woman complicates every thing. I think you would do as well to return to your house and stay there. Let us work this matter out in our own way."

She looked at him in surprise. There was a change in him from what he had been when Wilton first saw him. He was bold and defiant in his attitude, and he made no use of his imposing costume. She began to doubt him, and to wonder who he was. The knowledge he had of the past history of Dujardin puzzled her. It reminded her of a family story, which had been allowed to die away, in which Dujardin had been implicated in some way not complimentary to him.

"I can no go until I know he is safe," she said.

"I will let you know."

"Let me stay here."

"Impossible. They will suspect. These hounds may be spying about us now," he said.

"Then I must see him before I go."

"You had better not."

"I must!"

Anselmo closed the parlor door and drew the bolt. This done, he approached the fireplace, and touching a concealed spring in the wall, slid back a small panel and showed a dark opening. Putting in his head, he called in a low tone, and withdrew. In a moment the face of Wilton appeared in the opening.

"Hist," said Anselmo. "Be cautious now. Go close to him and whisper, mademoiselle."

He withdrew to a small room which opened into the parlor. The moment he was gone, hands and lips met, and they forgot every thing except that they were lovers. A half hour passed and Anselmo returned. He pushed Wilton back and closed the panel, ordering him to perfect silence.

"As for you, mademoiselle, your mission is ended here. Go back to your house, and let events shape themselves as they may."

CHAPTER V.

A DANGEROUS GAME.

THE soldier who had been left in charge by Major Dujardin was a keen and active villain, a fit instrument of his leader, who was himself suited to command such men. Deschappelles believed that Wilton was concealed somewhere on the premises, and that his promotion was certain if he could succeed in capturing him.

Few of the English scouts had dared to penetrate to the center of the city, but this young man, with an audacity truly wonderful, had succeeded in making himself acquainted with the secret places of the town, and in securing for himself an active and efficient aid, in the person of Andrew Despard.

Notwithstanding he had been for years working against the interests of France in Montreal, the finger of suspicion never had been pointed at Despard. There were many in the city who knew that he was about at unseemly hours, and in places where he had no right to be, but these were persons over whom he had acquired some power, which tied their tongues completely.

Soon after Marie left the house, the old man also left it, and ordered his servant to get his horse. It was now nearly noon, and the streets were full. Deschappelles made no objection to his departure; indeed, his absence was necessary to a little plan the soldier had marked out for himself. Anselmo rode at a round pace through the streets, and entered the quarter where Despard lived. In a short time he drew rein at the house. A sharp-looking boy came out of a small tenement across the street and led the horse away. The old man, after looking cautiously about him, rapped at the door. It was opened at once, and he entered. Shortly after, Andrew Despard came out, and walked quickly away. He did not pause until he reached the barracks, which were situated not far from the house of Anselmo. He inquired for Major Dujardin, and his inquiry was answered by the appearance of a smart-looking valet, who seemed a little discomposed upon seeing who the visitor was.

"Ah, Monsieur Despard?" he said.

"The same, Claude. I hope I see you in good health. I asked for your master, however."

"You can not see him just now; he is engaged."

"No matter; I wish to see him."

"It is impossible," persisted the servant.

"Nothing is impossible, my dear sir. I beg you will not make that weak-kneed statement again. Par example: you would not think I knew any thing of *your* private history."

"Nothing but good, I should hope, monsieur," said the valet, with a sanctimonious air.

"That is as it may appear. Different men look at such affairs in different lights. There is nobody about who can hear us?"

"Why do you ask?"

"Because I am about to make a statement which it would be better, perhaps, to keep from other ears than yours. My advice is, have no listeners; but that is as you please."

"There is no one near. What do you mean?"

"On the night of the 4th of January you took a walk quite late. On the corner of Nôtre Dame street, above the Fleur de Lis, you met a gentleman of the Hebrew persuasion, and went with him. You had a bundle under your arm. The Hebrew gentleman took you to a low shop. You unrolled the bundle and took from it the following articles."

He drew a paper from his pocket and read.

"One field glass, worth about two Louis——"

"*Mon Dieu!*" cried Claude.

"Two swords, one with a silver hilt, worth four Louis," he went on.

"*This man is the devil!*"

"A brace of dueling pistols, elegantly mounted, with the name of the owner on the hilt, worth at least four Louis d'or."

"*It is sorcery and nothing else*," moaned Claude, in despair.

"A handsome dagger, a Malay creese, a pair of blankets, a piece of handsome silk for a cloak pattern, and a quantity of miscellaneous property, worth in the aggregate twenty Louis.

All this property you sold to your Hebrew friend for six Louis. The swords and field glass brought two more."

"Ah, holy saints! I am undone forever! I am ruined, stock and block. You have come to impart this to my master?"

"That depends upon yourself," said Despard. "If you are of service to me, and do not grumble at the tasks I may give you, I shall take pleasure in keeping this to myself."

"Name your conditions."

"You shall give me, from time to time, a statement of your master's doings. I shall expect you to make notes of his in-comings and outgoings—to dog him upon occasions when he seems bent upon business of peculiar interest, and bring me word; to listen to his conversation when he is closeted with any one, no matter whom. I am not particular as to the matter on which they converse—any thing and every thing. Do you agree to this?"

"I have no option in the matter."

"Do it cheerfully or not at all."

"Cheerfully? Oh, I shall do it cheerfully enough. I have been accustomed to it, in fact. We servants expect to keep our masters under supervision, more or less. There is one thing monsieur has forgotten to mention. That point settled, it will be a pleasure to serve monsieur."

"And that?"

"The question of remuneration."

"Business-like and to the point. I like that. I have no doubt we shall get on famously together. You shall be well paid if you leave it to me. Another man might not pay you at all, having the power over you which I possess, but I like every thing to work harmoniously," said Despard.

"Thanks; monsieur will find me ready and willing," said Claude, eagerly.

"I shall expect it. Do not take the trouble to recognize me when we meet at any time, unless I require it. You see the necessity of that, I believe."

"It shall be as monsieur wishes."

"Then, for the first proof of your obedience, I wish to see your master."

"I will take in your name."

"Wait a moment."

Despard took a card from his pocket and wrote these words upon it :

"Doctor Despard wishes to see and converse with Major Dujardin. It will be for the interest of the major to see him."

Claude disappeared with the card. He was back directly, and invited Despard in. Dujardin was seated near a small table, and had been writing.

"Good-day to you, Monsieur Despard. You are welcome. Be seated. Claude, we do not need you."

Claude withdrew, and Dujardin turned his eyes on the face of the visitor, who met him by a keen, bold glance. Each seemed to read the other's purpose in his eyes. But the lapse of years had so changed Despard from the beardless stripling who had fought with Dujardin for the woman both loved, that the villain failed to recognize him.

"You escaped me last night," said Dujardin. "It was a lucky thing for you. As I hope to be saved—"

"Do you *really* hope that?" said Despard.

"Be careful, sir. I did not think you would have had the hardihood to seek me out, after what passed last night."

"It seems to me that the game is in my hands, sir. But, I do not come to quarrel with you. A friend of mine has been to me with a complaint that a guard has been placed in his house, without reason, by your orders."

"You mean the old student, called Anselmo?" asked Dujardin.

"Yes."

"I plead guilty. I placed a guard there, and there it shall remain until I am satisfied that the English spy is not concealed in the house."

"You are wrong, monsieur. It will not be well for you if the guard remains."

"Do you threaten me?"

"If you do not remove the guard, I will go to the Governor and lay bare before him your attempted outrage of last night."

"You would not dare do that."

"I see you do not know me. What have I to fear? My testimony, backed by that of mademoiselle, certainly is better

than your unsupported avowal. Besides, I have the word of
the guard, at whose appearance you gave up the pursuit. I
should also put upon oath your creatures, Langlier and Deschappelles, and it would go hard but the Judge Advocate
could wring some truth out of their lies."

"Who are you?"

"Andrew Despard, a loyal subject of France. Who are
you? I will tell you, for I know you well. You are a
man stained by a dozen crimes, and guilty of at least two
murders."

"Not so loud; for heaven's sake be more guarded," whispered Dujardin.

"Why should I be? Two murders? Three at least, and
perhaps four. For where is Terese D'Arcy and her lover?
You killed your poor tool, and then laid his blood upon guiltless shoulders. I know you but too well!"

"It seems that the very stars of Montreal are rising up
against me. This is the third man since last night who has
laid the guilt of murder on my head, and all of them have re-
ferred to a past which I deemed buried in oblivion. This
must not go on. You, at least, sh'll speak and tell me whence
this knowledge came."

"You will know in good time. I warn you, man, retri-
bution for past crimes may be long in coming, but sooner or
later it must find its place. Woe to you when all your crimes
are atoned for!"

"Are you man or devil? What do you ask of me?"

"The guard must be withdrawn from Anselmo's house."

"Is that all?"

"For the present, yes," replied Despard.

"You shall have what you ask; but do not think I
yield through fear of any thing you can do to me. If I believed that Wilton was still hidden in the house, you might
cut me into pieces before I would give an order withdrawing
the guard."

"It makes no difference what your motive be, so long as you
give the order. That will be enough for me. You think you
love the girl. Bah! you are foolish. You never loved any
thing so good and pure as Marie D'Arigny. I have long since
foresworn the happiness of woman's society. I never again

shall know the bliss of woman's love. But, such a creature as this warms my heart even now."

"You say I do not love her; the man who says that knows nothing of my heart."

"Did you love Terese D'Arcy?"

"Not exactly. It pleased me to break the romantic charm which bound her to that puling fool whom I hate, even now; but that he escaped his head must have fallen; I hope he is dead."

"Do you know where he is?" asked Despard, his eyes gleaming strangely.

"I never heard of him again. Where he went, no one knows. Perhaps he joined the stream of adventurers who came to this country. Certain it is, he never again set foot in Normandy. I think he is under the sod or the sea. Wherever he lies, the fiend go with his soul and have it in care."

"Then Terese escaped you?"

"She was a fool."

In an instant, with a mighty bound, Despard was upon the villain and had him by the throat. The countenance of the spy was distorted by passion, and his dark eyes flamed like newly-kindled fires. Then his fate was sealed, if the sudden fit of choler had not left Despard, as quickly as it came. He had bent the major backward over the chair on which he had been sitting, and the knife was lifted in air, but he paused. Whatever it might have been that stayed his hand, it is enough that he did not strike.

"Unsay that word, or you die!"

"Yes; don't strike me. I had no right to talk of her in that way," stammered Dujardin, pale with fear.

"Say she was good and pure."

"The angels are not more so."

Despard released him and he rose to his feet. The face of the spy was deadly pale. His fingers clenched and unclenched themselves as if he longed again to rush at the throat of the wretch whom he so hated. But he restrained himself.

"Where is Terese? Do you know?"

"I can not tell. She went mad, they say. I could not

help it. She fled. They found her mantle by the river-side, and a body was taken from the stream some miles below, and buried in the family tomb. You would not have dared to look upon her face, as she was there. I saw it, and, oh, mon Dieu! it was horrible."

"And you brought her to this! The good and innocent shall be avenged! But, no; your time is not yet. Write the order dismissing the guard."

"Will you take it?"

"Yes; I will give them their congé."

"It is better so. I am satisfied that they will do no good there."

He sat down and wrote: "On the receipt of this, Sergeant Deschappelles will return with his command to the barracks, where they will be put upon duty. It is not thought expedient to retain them in their present position.

"Signed, DUJARDIN, Major of Musketeers."

Despard took the paper and folded it up. While doing so, he kept his eyes on the face of Dujardin. He was evidently revolving some plot in his teeming brain.

"I can not tell where I have seen you, Monsieur Despard," he said. "It will come to me in time."

"I will tell you myself in a few days, if you care to know."

"I shall be charmed."

"I doubt it. Let me bid you good-day."

Claude was in the way as he passed out. A close observer might have seen something pass from hand to hand. However that might be, Claude was very drunk at the Fleur de Lis that night, and boasted that he had a way of getting plenty more gold pieces when these were gone. But no one could find out where his mine of wealth was.

Despard, after leaving the barracks, went at once to Anselmo's. As he neared the door he became conscious of a great confusion in the house. Throwing open the door, he broke in. The noise was from the upper part of the building. Drawing his sword, he leaped up the stairs.

The sight which greeted him was one to rouse the tiger in any man. Deschappelles had seized the old servant Annette and attached thumb-screws on each hand, to which one of his fellows gave a turn at every nod of the scoundrel's head. Just as Despard entered he was crying:

"Once for all I ask you, where is the spy hidden? If you answer, well. If she refuses, twist her thumbs off, boys!"

There was no sign of yielding on that firm old face. Despard was at the door. A lightning-like bound, the flash of a steel blade, and the ringleader lay weltering in his gore, while Despard, standing with one foot upon his chest, cried:

"Who comes next?"

No one stirred. There was no man among them hardy enough to face the deadly blade he wielded. There was something in his fierce face that awed them. Both men shrunk back, and muttered something about obeying orders.

"Take off those thumb-screws, then."

They obeyed without a word. The scarf which was bound over her mouth, to muffle her cries, was removed, and the woman, moaning with pain, dropped at his feet.

"Now let me hear what this outrage means, Caspar," said the avenger, pointing his reeking blade at one of the men. "Do not dare to hesitate. I will cut you down if you do not speak."

"It was Deschappelles, monsieur," replied the man. "He said that this spy, Wilton, was somewhere in the house, and that we could get it out of the woman if the old man went away. He left to complain to the Governor of our being here, and Deschappelles took the opportunity. It was not my fault if I obeyed orders. He was my superior."

"No man would take such an order. However, he has been punished. Take him up, and away with him. There are your orders. They come from Major Dujardin, and ought to be genuine. No words; leave the house."

"Take your foot off the sergeant, monsieur; he may have life in him."

"I hope so. I should not like to kill the hound, scoundrel though he is. Let me look at him. Bah! he is not badly hurt. Take him to the hospital. In three weeks he will be able to do the dirty work of some other man. He will never do any more for Mariot Dujardin ; let him be sure of that."

The men took the wounded wretch in their arms and carried him away. Despard sprung forward, lifted the poor old woman in his arms, and carried her to a couch on one side of the apartment. She revived in a moment, and lifting her swollen and discolored hands, burst into tears.

"Faithful creature," said Despard, "how you have suffered. Why was it done?"

"They might have cut me into pieces and I would never have told them where the young American was concealed. You came in time."

"You shall have your revenge for this, Annette. I have cleared the house of the villains. Now I must see Wilton."

CHAPTER VI.
A NIGHT'S WORK.

THE night came, and such a night as spies love, in which to do their work. As the darkness fell, Despard and Wilton stole out of the house together from the door in the rear, slipped over the wall, and stood in the next street. That night they had determined upon a perilous act. Private advices had warned them that the Governor and his Secretary that night left the castle for the outer lines, and that the Secretary bore upon his person papers which gave a list of the entire force of the French, under the Secretary's own hand. To possess these papers at all hazards, was the purpose of the two men. These in their hands, nothing need delay the advance of the English forces, now near at hand.

Onward through the silent street, they moved, the darkness falling upon them like a mantle. No one knew better than Despard how to elude the guards, for in his walk that morning he had passed over the very ground they were now traversing, and had noted the disposition of the men. He had

taken pains to instruct Wilton on these points, and the young
man knew the course before them.

They passed under the wall of a gloomy building at which
Wilton looked with considerable interest.

"You are looking at your late residence," said Despard,
laughing very low. "How did you like it?" (Wilton, as
stated, had been a prisoner on his previous visit to Montreal.)

"Not at all. It is not noted for the comfort it allows to
guests, and their rooms are rather narrow, and the beds hard.
It would have been the less endurable, but that the presence
of an angel lightened it."

"Being a lover, you of course can mean no other angel
than Marie D'Arigny."

"She visited me in the gloomy old place, when I was almost ready to despair. I do not care to describe my sensa-
tions when the door opened for her entrance. We had not
understood each other until then. Indeed, except for the
fact that I was in prison, and condemned to die, I might
never have spoken. But I could not help it then."

The building they were passing was the strong prison of
the post, in which Wilton had been confined, until saved by
the hands of Despard, Marie, and other friends.

"You would not like to go in and see your old room, I
suppose?"

"Not at all. Come on."

They relapsed into silence and walked on, side by side.
Though taking pains to avoid the guards, they did not succeed. Turning the corner of a street they came suddenly
upon a watch-fire. Before they could retreat they were chal-
lenged.

"What shall we do?"

"Impudence to our rescue. Come on. I have a pass for
myself and for you."

"Ha! How did you get it?"

"The Governor himself gave it to me upon my represent-
ing that I was a sort of doctor, practicing upon the poorer
class gratis. I do so, by the way."

"But my name."

"You shall see."

The sergeant in charge of the guard came forward. "Your names and stations, messieurs. Speak quickly."

Looking closely at the man, Despard saw that it was the same sergeant who had escorted himself and Marie to her residence, after he had snatched her from the hands of Dujardin and his vile assistants. This simplified matters immensely.

"Ah, good-evening, sergeant. I have not had an opportunity of thanking you for your good service to myself and the lady in my charge. Estephe, this is the sergeant who aided me in saving Marie D'Arigny."

"So it is yourself, Monsieur Despard. I give you good-evening. But you must have a pass."

"Certainly. Here it is."

The sergeant took the paper and read it by the firelight.

"The pass is good," said the sergeant. "Pass on!"

They left the watch-fire behind them before Wilton spoke. "I do not understand how he passed me so readily."

"It is simple enough. The pass is for Doctor Despard and his assistant, Estephe Varny. Your name, for the present, is Estephe Varny. Do you understand?"

Wilton laughed. "I change my name so often while in Montreal, that, upon my word, I hardly know sometimes what I am called. But have your way. Ha! Who is that?"

Though it was dark, they could make out the figure of some person passing by, walking in the center of the street. Just then a light flashed from the window of a house near at hand, and lighted up the figure. They could see that it was a woman. Despard caught a glimpse of a part of the face only; the rest was muffled in a heavy cloak.

"Stop," said he. "For God's sake, let me see your face."

"Away," said a clear, rich voice. " s you are a man, touch me not. I call on you, sir, as a gentleman, to see that your friend does not put his hand upon me."

"It is a voice from the grave," faltered Despard. "My dear lady, do not fear harm from me. There is little to fear from a broken man, who, having lost all which made life dear to him, has lived for no object but to be revenged on those who have wronged him. Fear me not, lady."

"I do not fear you. I know you well. You are the man

they call Andrew Despard. But that is not your true
name."

"Who are you?" he cried, starting forward impulsively.
She waved him back.

"It is not for you to know this, Andrew Despard. It is
enough that I am near you, and that I, at least, will never
reproach you for what you have done."

"You speak in the voice of one who is gone," said
Despard, in broken tones. "I could almost be mad enough
to think she lived yet, but that my faithful old servant swore
to me that she is dead."

"Let me pass," said the woman, in deep agitation. "I
must not be stopped."

"Shall I see you again?"

"I know not. Yes. Let me go now. But stay. You
go to-night upon a dangerous mission."

"How know you that?"

"Ask me no questions. It is enough for you to know this
that there are those to whom your words and ways are not so
deep a secret as you may imagine. There are those who
have seen you in all your disguises, and I am one of them."

"You are not my enemy, or I should have been betrayed."

"Not your enemy," she answered, sadly. "Ah, no; not
that. Be careful to-night. I will not say, give up your de-
sign. That would be asking too much. But do not expose
yourself unnecessarily."

"I will not," said Despard. "You have my promise."

"Thanks; good-night then."

As she moved away, they saw some one join her, and the
two hurried down the street together. Wilton had been
somewhat startled at the meeting with this woman and her
knowledge of his companion.

"Do you know her?" he asked.

"I could not see her face," said Despard, almost angrily.
"Why should she conceal it? The voice seemed familiar.
Why is it that I think so much of Teresa lately? I can
not understand it. She is dead. Years have passed since
the waters of the Seine closed over her beautiful head. Bear
down such thoughts. Bury them deeper than Prospero sunk
his books. Vengeance only is my work. I do not"

A change came over the face of the spy and he was again the hardy, keen, determined man. He led the way at a quick pace, until they reached a point in the long street whence a dark and narrow alley opened upon the main road. In this alley they took their stand and waited. Both were closely masked, and stood leaning on their drawn swords, waiting for their prey.

They had not long to wait. Scarcely ten minutes had passed when two men came down the street together, picking their way cautiously over the stony path.

"Let me hear them speak," said the spy. "Then I can tell whether they are our men or not."

"Peste!" cried one of the new-comers, "If I could have my way there would be no such night-journeys as these. A curse upon these English! They make our lives a burden. I pray the day may come quickly when they shall either be driven out of the country, or we. One or the other must happen in the end."

"Certainement," said his companion, with the French grimace and shrug. "It will come too soon."

"Our men," whispered Despard. "Take the Secretary; I will attend to the Governor."

There is little time lost when a daring deed is to be done by such men. The French guards were not five squares away. Despard threw himself upon the Governor, and flung a heavy scarf over his head, muffling him so completely that an outcry was next to impossible. Wilton was not so fortunate with the Secretary. That worthy, a muscular though slightly-built man, eluded the first rush, and actually got his sword partly out of its sheath. There was no help for it, and Wilton knocked him down instantly.

"Away with them," whispered Despard. "There is no time to lose."

The prisoners were gagged and blindfolded. Despard whistled in a low key. Four men emerged from several hiding-places and came forward. They evidently understood their business, for, without question, they separated—two of them taking up the Governor, and the others the Secretary, and hurried down the alley. When the Governor's eyes next saw the light he was sitting in a chair, bound tightly, *vis-à-vis* with his able friend, the Secretary. The room in which they sat was a low-roofed, rude place, evidently the dwelling of one of the lower order. Two more utterly confounded men than these probably could not have been found in the colony of Canada.

"What does this mean?" said the Governor.

"Parbleu! I should say some one of his majesty's subjects proposed to give us lodgings for the night, gratis."

"Is this a time to jest, D'Aumale? I am astonished."

"So am I, your excellency," said the incorrigible Secretary, "deeply surprised. I am also grieved that you have men in the colony so base that they do not respect the person of the Governor, nor of that worthy man, the Governor's Secretary. Our surprise, however, can not aid us in the least. Then there is nothing for it but to follow the phraseology of our excellent friends the English, and 'grin and bear it.' Aha! here is our captor."

The door opened, and Despard, still masked, appeared upon the threshold. In one hand he held a pistol, the long, bright barrel of which glittered in the rays of the lamp he carried. He spoke to them in English, the better to conceal his identity.

"Good-night to you, sir. My friend, the Secretary, I'm right glad to see yer."

"I can not speak well your execrable language," said the Secretary, in French.

"Speak it as well as you kin, then. You can't expect an Englishman to understand your cursed lingo. You've got papers we want. I've come to find them."

"If you would release my hands I would save you that trouble," said the Governor.

"So would I, vraiment. Let me speak wiz Monsieur Anglais. Be composed. Release my hands, ven I vill give you une, deux, trois papier; ze whole plan of ze campaign," said the Secretary.

"D'Aumale, will you turn traitor?" cried the Governor.

"Pardonnez-moi, Monsieur le Governor," said the Secretary. "It is useless to resist. Zis gentlehomme vill release my hands, and I vill proceed to give him ze papier. Oui; vraiment."

"Oh, shut up, Frenchy," said Despard, adopting to a nicety the rough phrases and rude ways of an English forester. "We ain't goin' to listen to no nonsense; we ain't goin' to take none from you: now mind that. You ain't goin' to git your hands free, neither; so just you hold still."

"Peace, D'Aumale," said the Governor. "This is only one of these rough Englishmen, who think there is a merit in rudeness. Perhaps I can do something with him. Attend to me, monsieur. Do you know who I am?"

"I rather think I *do*," said Despard.

"Then you know I am Governor of this colony?"

"Yes."

"You are a spy in the service of England. It is a poor service. The work is hard and the pay but little. It is in your power, at one stroke, to gain all the wealth you will require, and at the same time escape from this degrading service."

"How ken I do it, mister?"

"By setting me at liberty, and informing me of the position and plans of the enemy. For this service I will pay you more than all your years of hardship—for a man of such address as you must have been a long time a scout—have ever paid you. For your own good, think of this offer a moment."

"How much?"

"Three hundred guineas, in your own currency: a great sum."

"What's the use of talkin'?" said Despard. "It can't be done! I won't take your money. You shut up. You can't tempt me, if I *am poor*. Nobody but a low, dirty monseer would have tried it on an honest man."

"Mille diables!" shouted D'Aumale, writhing in his bonds, "is dat ze vay you speak to ze Governor? By St. Denis, if I had my hands free I vould kill you. Oui. I can not parlez your language. If I talk him vell, it vould give me great plaisir to—what you call him?—sw'ar you in good Anglais. I can speak seven oder language, but I can not speak your Anglais vell."

"We only speak *one* language here, and mighty little of *that*," said Despard, pressing the muzzle of his pistol to the forehead of the Secretary. "Move, whisper, or look at me again, and I spatter your brains upon the wall. Come yere, you. Go through this chap's clothes."

Wilton, yet closely masked, entered the room and began to search the Secretary. They found in his pockets various articles which only a Frenchman would carry. Lumps of white sugar, a small flask of *eau de vie*, a snuff-box, and at last a package of papers.

"Open 'em, and see if they are the ones you are arter," said Despard.

Wilton obeyed. Opening the first paper he began to read, translating into English. It was addressed to the "Divinity of Montreal," Marie D'Arigny.

"Why, you soup-eating heathen," cried Wilton, "I have a mind to cram this production down your throat."

"What? Cram him down my t'roat? ze song I write in honuaire of ze maid I love? I s'all demand satisfaction from you—ze satisfaction of a gentleman! You s'all meet me, sar, wiz any weapon you chose, and I vill make you take back ze word you 'ave use. Cram? I s'all 'ave ze grand plaisir of cut your t'roat from ear to ear."

"Nonsense!" ejaculated Wilton.

"I s'all remember zese insult. Ze grand satisfaction can only suffice. You s'all name your place and weapons. You s'all give me your card. If you refuse, I s'all say you are un lâche. You understand?—un lâche extraordinaire. Ah! Parbleu!"

"I have no time to quarrel with you now," said Wilton. "Perhaps we shall never meet again. But, if we do, I promise you the satisfaction you ask. These are not the papers we want. As far as I can see, they are private papers."

"Keep 'em," said Despard, observing that the eyes of the Secretary began to brighten. "There may be something among 'em. Let me look him over. You hold the pistol. If he says any thing, blow out his brains."

Despard ran his hands over the person of the Secretary, and found nothing whatever. The Governor began to smile. The Secretary had taken some precaution before coming out, it was evident. Despard was a little puzzled. He stooped to look at the shoes of the Secretary, and in doing so, laid his hand upon his knee. To his surprise, he felt something hard under his hand. D'Aumale began to curse in choice Gascon, of which he was master. Despard only laughed, and drawing a knife, in spite of the struggles and protestations of the Frenchman, cut a hole in the unmentionables of the Secretary, and found a small pocket just behind the knee, in which was a thin tin case or box. He opened it, and found several papers, closely packed.

"All right," he said; "this is important or he'd never hev hid it so close. You look at 'em."

Wilton ran his eye hastily over the papers.

"Just the thing," he said. "It's all right; nothing more to be done."

"Whatever may happen, monsieur," said the Governor, "*you* can not deceive me. I know your voice and figure."

"And whom do you think me?"

"You are the man known as the Silent Slayer. You are the man who was taken at the castle and escaped from prison."

"Ha! ha!" said Wilton, unmasking. "My dear Governor, how are you? I have not had the pleasure of seeing your face for some time."

"I was right, then. Beware, young sir! Hardihood may go too far. You will yet be laid by the heels."

"I may be, my dear sir. It will happen in spite of all we can do, perhaps. At present you are in my hands. What is to hinder me from killing you?"

"Nothing; I am in your power. Do with me as you will," said the Governor, sullenly.

"It may be forced upon me. If—"

What he meant to say was lost in a terrible crash, as the door was beaten in. Despard seized the Governor by the arm, and held a pistol to his head. Wilton grasped the Secretary in the same manner, and not a moment too soon, for over the threshold poured a dozen of the guards, holding their bayonets at the charge. Behind them the savage face of Muriot Dujardin could be seen. The soldiers halted as they saw the attitude of the two spies, and Dujardin pushed through them to the front.

"Halt!" cried Wilton.

Even Marlot turned pale. Although the face of Despard was covered, there was something in their attitudes which told their determination, even before Wilton spoke.

"Advance one foot," he said, in a voice whose condensed firmness there was no mistaking, "and these men die!"

"You dare not do it," said the other; "my men would cut you into pieces."

"Do not put it to the test," cried Wilton, cocking his pistol. Despard did the same. There is nothing pleasant in the click of a pistol-lock, when the muzzle is not three inches from your head. The Governor found it so.

"Wait a moment, Major Dujardin. Let us treat with these men. They are evidently desperadoes," said the Governor, in some trepidation.

"They are indeed, your excellency."

"We are in a position to dictate terms," said Wilton; "my friend will give them to you."

"It's just yer," said Despard, still keeping the dialect of a frontier man. "They've got to git out of this, and give us a fair start. All we ask of this Frencher is to take out his men and form 'em in line at the end of the street. Then we will do as we choose."

"Confusion! We will not agree," cried the Governor.

"Very good. You will at once perceive that this is our only chance. If we are taken, we *hang*. That is understood. So, if you are tired of life, order yer men to come on."

"You surely would not murder us?"

"We've got our lives to save. Don't git it into your head that we won't pull triggers, because we *will*. I reckon you had better order these chaps out."

"Major Dujardin," said the Governor, "form your men at the end of the street."

The guards trooped out. Despard called the major back.

"Say, hadn't you better call away the men at the windows?"

"Men at the windows! Who said I had men there?"

"It don't matter in the least; only we want 'em away," said the spy.

"It shall be done. I don't know you, my man, but you are a sharp one."

"I counted your men before they went out, you know. You ken go."

Dujardin strode away.

The moment he was gone Despard leaped to the window, and threw it open. The night was dark as night could well be, but he could hear men moving in the rear of the house. A silent signal to Wilton was all he needed. With a pistol in one hand, and a sword in the other, Despard led the way through the *front* door. No one had expected him there, and, though one or two of the guard were loitering about, they were powerless to stop the two men, who rushed by them like the wind. The guard entered the house, and released the Governor and Secretary. Woe to Wilton if they caught him now!

CHAPTER VII.

A FACE IN THE WALL.

THE versatile valet of Mariot Dujardin was not in the least annoyed by finding himself in the power of Despard, when he knew that it would *pay* him. Betraying his master was nothing new to him, and he set about it with a zest. He had followed the major on the night when the Governor and Secretary were seized, and from a nook in the wall had managed to watch the proceedings without being seen. When the two men escaped he was about to follow, but second thought told him that this course was useless, as they would doubtless take him for a pursuer and avoid him. He did the next best thing; he crept near and listened to the conversation between the Governor and Dujardin.

"How came you to arrive so opportunely, Mariot?" asked the Governor.

"I had set one of my men to watch the house of the old

student, Anselmo. He saw two men leave the house by the rear entrance and followed them. After seeing them posted in an alley, evidently waiting for some one, he ran to the barrier and gave the alarm."

"Ha! They came from the house of the student?" said the Governor.

"Yes, your excellency."

"Strange. He seems a simple, kind old man. What should this Wilton do at his house?"

"I can not tell. He was there last night, I am certain," replied Dujardin.

"Why so?"

"One of my men saw him in the window and reported him. I went to take him, but he was nowhere to be found. Doubtless he was concealed somewhere at the time."

"Are you sure your man knew him?"

"Certainly. He had put out his head to close a shutter, when Langlier passed upon the walk, so close that their faces almost touched. I repeat, it was the very man. No one knows him better than Langlier."

"That same rogue deserves a halter himself," said the Governor. "You remember that he attacked Lamont and this same Wilton in the wood above the Chambly. I should have hung him for that, but for you, Mariot. I wonder you keep the fellow about you."

"He is useful to me," said Dujardin. "I grant you he is a villain. What shall we do in regard to this old man?"

"He must be taken. Send your men under a sergeant, and bring him to head-quarters."

Dujardin turned to execute the order. Claude had heard all he required, and ran away like the wind, taking the direction of the house of Anselmo. As he ran, he stumbled over some one who was in the path, a stunted, shriveled figure, who cursed him in good French for the act.

"Beware what you do!" he cried. "No man ever did a wrong to Conrad Dumont who did not at some time repent it."

"Are you Conrad, the sorcerer?" asked Claude, rising. "I must speak to you. Do you know Despard?"

'I have heard of him."

Nonsense. He is a friend of yours. I am one of his agents. He must have told you before this.'

" Your name?"

" Claude Tollisson."

" The valet of Mariot Dujardin?"

" Oui, monsieur," said the valet.

" Very good. You are on the list of our paid agents. What have you to impart? Speak, and let your words be to the point."

" They shall be. A guard has been sent to seize the man known as Anselmo, the student. If you have any interest in him, give him warning. Have I done well to tell you?"

" Excellent. You could not have done better. Away with you, and watch your master like a lynx. I will engage that Anselmo shall not be taken."

The moment Claude turned away, the deformed one started on a run, showing an agility which no one would have believed possible in a man of his form. Away through the dark streets, through alleys where the water stood in stagnant pools, he never slackened his headlong speed until he saw before him the house of Anselmo. Annette came to the door in answer to his rap and he passed in.

When the guard came to capture Anselmo, he was not to be found. The old servant could not tell where he had gone, or at what hour he would return. There was nothing for it but to wait, so they ordered the servant up stairs, and took possession of the lower part of the house.

It was not yet day, and the room in which the soldiers sat 'ooked gloomy enough under the waning light of the single taper the servant gave them. The soldiers, stout-hearted fellows enough, in their way, could endure most things in campaigning, but the gloomy old house struck a chill into their very marrow.

" They say the old place is haunted," said one. " Ghosts flit to and fro in the night. Kaspar says he saw the devil sitting on the ridge-pole one night, grinning at the moon."

" It might well be true," said another. " A curse upon the old crib. You know me, Pierre, don't you? Parbleu !

I am not a man to be easily frightened, but I am not in love with that old rack-a-bones of a house. They say the old man is a pestilent astrologer."

"Can he read the fates?"

"They say so. If he could, he would be no worse than this Conrad Dumont, who lives in the little white house at the barrier. You should have heard him talk to some of the lads the other night. If any of them had been so unfortunate as to have cut a throat or lifted a watch in his time, who should know it but Conrad, and jeer at them on account of this little incident? Upon my word it was awful. I was the only honest man in the party, and yet he gave *me* a benefit too."

"I have seen him," said Pierre. "A distorted lump. A cold-blooded, vindictive, cruel-hearted ape."

"Ha! ha! ha!" shrieked a voice near them. "Hark to the devils. Speak well of your betters."

Every man sprung to his feet and grasped his gun. But, no enemy was in sight. The sergeant darted to the door and flung it open. As he did so, a perfect yell of savage laughter filled the room. Yet the halls were empty, and there was only one other door opening into the room. One of the men pushed it open with his foot and showed a small bedroom. He poised his bayonet to thrust at the person who had broken in on their discourse, and darted into the little room, fully persuaded that he had trapped the fellow at last. But, to his surprise, the room was empty, and a shrill voice seemed to ring in his very ears.

"Conrad Dumont! A distorted lump! Ha! ha! ha! Who could help laughing when he sees a lot of villains such as these tramping to and fro upon forbidden ground? The devils laugh. The owls hoot. The white owl, sitting in his tree by the door, cries out, tu-whoo!"

A paleness settled upon the faces of the soldiers as they looked from one to another. What could this mean? No one was in sight, and yet the cries seemed to fill the very room.

"'Hell is empty, and all the devils are here,'" quoted the sergeant, who was a literary character. "Up stairs with you, Jason and Danton. We will see if the soldiers of the guard are the men to be insulted by clap-trap and astrology. It shall not be. Up with you. Search every room through and through. Leave not a nook or corner unexplored, no matter where. Kill any thing that comes in your way."

The two soldiers sprung up the stairs with fixed bayonets, and burst into the rooms above. They found no one but Annette, who stood on the landing, trying to find out the cause of the tumult below.

"For heaven's sake, gentlemen, remember that I am alone here, and rely upon your generosity. You shall have all you require, only do not be too loud."

"Out of the way, old lady," replied one of the guard. "No harm is intended you, but we must find who it is that dares to shout in derision at the soldiers of the guard."

"Have you heard the shouts? Ah, woe is me, the sad times have come again to the house of my master! Sorrow we have had, and now it is here again," said Annette.

"What do you mean?" cried the leading soldier. She answered by a look of terror.

"You do not, can not know the secrets of the house. Did it seem a gibing, bitter spirit; a mocking, cruel ghost?"

"We heard some vile wretch jeering at us," replied the soldier, "and we will not endure it. Stand aside, for we will search for it."

"Go on, if ye will," said Annette. "If ye come to harm, lay not the blame on my guiltless head."

They pushed open the door of the room directly over the place where they had been sitting when the first alarm sounded, and entered. It was a square, plastered apartment, without furniture of any kind. The bare white walls had a dreary and uninviting look. As they gazed about them the same elfish laugh which had astonished them before sounded in their ears, and they saw, in the gloom at the back of the room, a face hideous in every lineament, looking out of the solid wall. Even as they saw it, a screech like a panther's seemed to shake the room. The man bearing the torch dropped it, while his companion stood there powerless to raise his rifle. Annette darted in and picked up the flaming torch.

"Are you satisfied?" she cried. "Come away, before a worse thing happen to you. I warn you."

"Did you see it, Danton?" gasped one. "Dieu de batailles! Did you ever see the like? Ugh! I am in a very jelly from fear. I own it. If the rest saw what we have seen, they would leave this accursed house."

"Yah-h-h-h-ah!"

A prolonged yell broke in upon the speaker, and they saw the same distorted, fiend-like face which they had seen before. The man called Jason lifted his musket with a shaking hand, and pulled the trigger. When the smoke cleared away, Danton snatched the torch from the hand of Annette, and darted forward. He knew that his companion was a deadly shot, and hoped that the thing who had so terrified them had got its deserts. Reaching the spot, he saw nothing but the round hole in the paneled wall, where the bullet had pierced it. By this time the others were in the room, looking with astonishment at the face of Danton, who was deadly pale.

"Say what you will, lads," quoth he. "I never believed in ghosts. But, when I see them with my own eyes, I can not doubt the evidence of my senses. Jason will swear, and so will I, that he fired at a face looking out of the wall at this very spot. This good woman can tell you the same."

"Liars, thieves, scum of the world," cried the same shrill voice. "Fire at *me*; fire at a cloud. I'm a devil! Yah-h-h-ah!"

"God help us, what necromancy is this?" cried the sergeant. "We have fallen upon a strange thing. I never saw the like in all my life. By the soul of my body, it is wonderful. However, here we are and here we stay until the man they call Anselmo sees fit to return. Jason and Danton, you will remain in this room. Have your arms ready for use. Pierre and Cartier, take the room below. As for myself, I shall remain at the door."

They took their posts without demur. Whatever her faults as a nation, as a military one France is superb. Her soldiers are the very essence of obedience. These men were terrified, it is true; but, they took their places firmly, and waited for events to shape themselves as they would.

The sergeant was a bold man. He had fought the battle

of his country in many lands and had grown gray in the service. A lieutenancy had been promised him, but he had refused it, on the ground that his education was not sufficient for the purpose. He carried a little table into the hall before the door, drew his sword and laid it before him together with his pistols, cocked and laid with the butts toward his hand, ready to grasp at a moment's notice. Annette had brought him a flask of Burgundy, and he sat there, trifling with his glass, and trying to study out the riddle of the old house.

"Queer," muttered the sergeant. "I don't understand this at all."

Perhaps an hour had passed. It was nearly daylight, but in that portion of the night when objects seem to loom up through a mist. At that hour the sergeant received a shock. The door of the room in which his men were posted was closed. He was in a half-doze, when a brawny hand was suddenly clapped upon his mouth and he was thrown upon the floor. Looking up, he saw the point of a knife at his throat, and like an old campaigner gave up with a good grace. His captor was Wilton, who, now that he had been recognized, kept his face uncovered. Behind him stood Despard, still masked. Leaving the sergeant in charge of Despard, Wilton stepped lightly to the door and locked the two soldiers in. He had already taken the precaution to fasten the blinds on the outside. This done he went up the stairs and locked the other two, while Despard stood laughing.

"Now that the birds are safely caged," said Wilton, "let us to business. Call Annette."

She came down quickly, looking pleased at seeing the sergeant extended on his back, held in abeyance by the knife of Despard, who frowned at him ominously when he attempted to rise.

"How came these fellows here?" he demanded.

"They came to take my master prisoner. Two men were seen to leave the house last night and were followed."

"Ah-ha. So that was the way of it? Our friends keep a good watch over us. Thanks to a good friend, they did not take us napping. How have these men treated you?"

"They are not like the gang Dujardin sent before," said

Annette. "They used me as well as was consistent with duty."

"I am glad to hear it. These are soldiers. I myself have been in the service of France. Rise, sir. I am sorry we were compelled to throw you down rather roughly."

"It is the fortune of war," said the sergeant. "We can not help ourselves."

"We must bind you to the chair," said Wilton.

He was tied hand and foot. Soon, the men locked in the rooms began to realize that they were in trouble, and commenced to kick at the doors. Without paying any attention to them, Despard left the room, and was heard walking about in the rooms above. He shortly appeared, with a package in his hand.

"You must abandon the rest, then," said Wilton. "Will Anselmo return?"

"I fear that you will never see his face again," said the other, with a peculiar smile.

They passed out of the house, and to Wilton's surprise were followed by Annette, who only went as far as the gate of the D'Arigny mansion. As they halted a moment to bid her good-by, a man came up to them. It was Conrad. His face was absolutely distorted by elfish laughter and he chuckled as he stood before them.

"Conrad, you should not be out on such a night as this," said Despard.

"Who but I? If you had seen what I saw this night, you would laugh as I do. They thought the devil was after them, sure."

"You have been frightening the soldiers," said Despard; "I see that."

"Out of their five senses," replied Conrad, with another chuckle. "To see them standing there, the color of bleached cloth, and not laugh, was impossible. Annette aided me. Good-night, Annette."

The woman went to the door in the rear of the house, which had evidently been left open for her, and entered. The others passed on. Next day Annette was arrested by order of the Governor, and brought to the castle for examination. Nothing of interest could be elicited. Of her master she could not or would not tell any thing. Where he had gone, whence he had come, when he would return, all was in the dark. She knew nothing of the men who had come into the house. They were strangers to her, she avowed. She denied all the statements of the sergeant, *in toto;* said that the Burgundy she had set before him was very strong, and she should not be surprised if that had something to do with his strange powers of invention. She was at last released and allowed to return; but she went back to Marie, not to Anselmo's house.

CHAPTER VIII.

DUJARDIN'S VISIONS.

MARIOT DUJARDIN, on the night following the trial of the old servant, went out alone. That is, he supposed so, when, in reality his trusty servant was close at his heels, watching every step he took, slinking around the corners of dark streets, stopping when he stopped, and again going forward when he pursued his way. He stopped at last before a house which stood by itself, gloomy and dark; he rapped at the door, and it swung open, apparently without human agency, for no servant appeared. There was something in the mysterious and silent manner in which the door opened and swallowed up the major, which awed the servant, and he halted in the street and looked rather nervously at the mysterious door. As he stood there, a voice sounded in his ear; at the same moment a firm hand fell upon his shoulder.

"You watch Dujardin," said the voice.

Astonished by the assertion, Claude could only stammer, without making any connected reply.

"Do not deny it. Enter here, I give you leave; for I take it you are no friend of Dujardin."

"Enter where?"

"At yonder door."

"I do not know the occupants of the house."

"You need not, sir. Pass on unquestioned. Within yonder house you will be safe, so long as you follow and watch

no one but your master. Pause not, turn not to the right
hand nor to the left, follow no one else, and it shall be well
with you."

Claude entered the mysterious door. As his hand touched
it, he saw the heavy oak swing back upon its hinges to admit
him, and then close as noiselessly as before. The hall in
which he stood was very dark, and to his surprise and terror
a cold, clammy hand was laid upon his wrist and drew him
forward. He began to wish he had not been so officious in following his master.

"What do you want?" he muttered.

"Speak not," said a low but terribly savage voice. "Your
life is in peril. Hear me. Within this house, I charge you,
as you value life and happiness, speak not, but obey."

Claude was trembling like an aspen leaf; but there was no
retreat for him now. He had nothing to do but to follow his
leader, whoever it might be. He was led through long passages of the dark house, fearing each moment to receive a
dagger in his heart, until he came suddenly to a place where
a light streamed through an opening in the wall.

"Look," said his conductor. "Your master is here.
Watch him through this opening."

Satisfied that he was not to be injured, Claude set about
his duty with new zest. He looked through the opening.
Dujardin was pacing up and down the narrow room, apparently waiting for some one, and at the same time undecided
what course to take. His face looked gloomy under
the lamps. He had been unsuccessful in all his attempts
lately. Some one had met and foiled him at every turn.
A hidden influence, whose he could not divine, had been
at work. That day he had received a note, couched in these
words :

"If Marlot Dujardin would know why he has been so
unfortunate of late, let him come to the Rue Bartolemy,
near the river. The house will be shown him when he reaches
the street."

Tossed about by doubts and fears, Dujardin followed even
these vague directions, and had been admitted.

The room in which he sat was a beautiful one—a very
miracle of taste. The carpets were so soft that the feet sunk

into them at every step. Sofas, ottomans and the like, covered with rich velvet, were scattered about the great room, and pictures of rare beauty covered the walls. But he was in no mood to notice the beauty of the room. A look of annoyance passed over his face as some moments went by, and no one appeared.

All at once Claude became conscious that some one else beside the major was in the room—a woman, in a flowing robe of white, her face concealed by a thick lace mask.

"You have come at our bidding, Mariot Dujardin," said a voice like a flute, so sweet and clear was it. "I have promised you the reason of your late trouble; you shall see me keep my word. You are satisfied that some influence has been working against you, lately?"

"Who are you?" said Dujardin. "Let me see your face."

"Dog!" cried the woman, fiercely; "dare so much as to lay a finger upon my robe, and you die. Beware!"

"Oh, as to that, you can not frighten me, my lady. However, as you choose to remain incog., it shall be as you say. To your work; do as you have promised."

"Keep your eyes upon yonder wall," said the woman.

He obeyed her. In a moment a strange whiteness appeared upon the wall, and then light and shade began to show themselves; directly after, a picture appeared. It represented a grove in summer. A youth and maiden were walking down a sunny path, hand in hand, while another young man, half-hidden by the bushes, was peeping out at them with an angry eye. Dujardin started and turned pale, for in the countenance of the skulking man he recognized himself, and in the others, two of his victims.

"You know them, I see," said the lady. "This is the first picture of your life; let it fade."

As she spoke a shadow began to fall upon the picture. Each moment it grew less distinct, and in a moment more n ng was seen but the bare white wall.

"This is jugglery," said Dujardin. "I did not come here to see it; and I will not remain. Go your own way; I leave the house this moment."

"Remain!" said a deep voice.

He turned, and saw a man of tremendous stature, holding in his hand a heavy club, which he swung high above his head.

"Have I been decoyed here to be murdered?" shrieked Dujardin.

"No, villain. We are not of your kind. Look to it that you remain until we have done with you."

"You may retire now, Gabriel," said the lady. "He will stay to see the other pictures of his life."

The shadows again began to fall upon the wall, and showed another scene. A duel in a crowded room; a group of young men, most of them in the uniform of the French service, formed in a circle, and in the midst the combatants. One of them was down, and the other was standing over him, wiping his bloody sword. The face of the man upon his back was that of Dujardin.

"You see this?" said the woman, in a thrilling voice.

"Yes," said he, in a half-whisper.

"It is well. Let the picture pass, and another come."

Again the shadows came upon the picture, and it was gone. They came quickly now. As the third fell upon the wall, Dujardin uttered a yell of absolute terror, and covered his eyes. A man was bending over another, who lay dead upon the road. The face of the dead man was half-concealed from sight; but that of the murderer was in plain view; it was that of Dujardin!

"Fiend, devil in woman's form," he cried. "Who are you, and how dare you rake from the depths of the past the story of old days, and bring it up like this? It is a foul lie. Who has dared to make me their sport in this way?"

"Peace, fool! you know not what you say. I have shown you a true picture of your life in France. You can not deny it with truth. I could show you more. I could bring you pictures from a long life of guilt. I could show you burning cabins, and old men and women thrown on the blazing rafters. I could show you brave young D'Arigny, murdered by your hands."

"Now, by my patron saint, who could stand idly and bear such insults as these, does not deserve the name of man.

Where is my sword? Give me but that, and then bring in your ruffian brawlers, one at a time, and I will face them."

"The redeeming quality in your bad life, Marlot Dujardin, is a certain kind of bravery. You do not fear death, but only because you believe death to be annihilation. Your sword shall be returned to you soon, when you have leave to depart. At present, I have something more to show you."

"I will see no more."

"You must; you spend a part of the night in this house. You shall be safe. I promise that. But if you see sights which make your false heart quake, as you *shall* see them, it will be because you are guilty of innocent blood. Yonder is a room. Pass in, and spend the hour in sleep, if you can."

"I will not."

"Beware, I tell you. If you refuse, I will have you seized and chained to the bed. Take care you do not force me to do this, or you may have cause to repent it."

"What right have you to detain me?"

"The right of the stronger; you are in my power," she said.

"I'll not endure it."

"Go, then. I do not oppose you. Leave the house."

He turned to go away; but, to his surprise, no door was to be seen. Except on the side upon which the pictures had been shown, which was white, the room was paneled in oak. But, in the hundred panels, who could tell where the door stood?

"At least I have *you* here," he cried, seizing her suddenly. "Your body shall be my ransom."

"Gabriel, appear!" she cried.

As she said this, Dujardin received a terrible blow, which felled him to the earth, senseless. When he rose to his feet, he found the blood trickling from a wound in his forehead. He was alone in the room; no, not alone, for ghostly forms seemed to flit about him on every hand, and, even as he looked, the wall of the room lightened suddenly, and he saw another picture.

It represented the bank of a river, in a place where reeds
and ferns grew. In the distance rose the towers of some
great city. But the foreground of the picture was the terrible past. There, half concealed by the water, with her abun-
dant tresses floating out upon the waves, lay a woman whom
he remembered but too well. That drowned face was one
which he had cared for in his time, for it was that of Terese
D'Arcy, the lost bride of Despard.

These horrible pictures were too much even for the iron
soul of Dujardin. He ran round the room despairingly, clutching at the walls and beating at the panels, crying out for
mercy, begging them in the name of the saints to let him out,
to go away from such horrible sights and scenes. It was only
answered by a mocking laugh. He turned, and there, standing close to the wall, clad in the white habiliments of the
grave, stood the exact counterpart of the pictured face. She
was pointing one white arm at the picture, and the other at
him. The wretched man uttered a despairing yell, and fell
prostrate upon the floor, clutching at the carpet. When he
looked up again, the picture was gone from the wall, and the
figure had disappeared. In its place stood the tall form of
Gabriel.

"Rise," he said. "You have seen enough. You know
now why it is that you have not succeeded in your enterprises
of late. It is because God will not suffer such a guilty wretch
to live. Your time is drawing near."

"Am I to go now?"

"Yes; unless you would like to see another picture."

"For heaven's sake, do not speak of it," he gasped.

"Speak not of heaven, irreverent scoffer. Go; and see to
it that you do not enter this street again."

"No need to tell me that," said the villain, trembling. "I
shall keep clear of it. I was a fool to come here in the first
place."

"You are right; it would have been better for you if you
had stopped away. Come."

He took the major by the hand and led the way out of the
hall and into the street. Here he received his sword, and was
suffered to depart. The innate villainy of his heart was such
that after receiving the weapon, he turned to thrust it into the

back of Gabriel as he mounted the steps. But that worthy man had faced about and stood on his guard.

"Go!" he said. "You will not kill me to-night."

With a muttered curse, Dujardin thrust his sword into the scabbard, and walked away. He had not gone half a dozen blocks when two men passed him. As they did so, he heard the name of Marie spoken by one of them. He was a man who never forgot a face or figure, and looking closely at the speaker, even in the darkness he thought he could make out the form of Wilton. Approaching them, he took the privilege, as officer of the night, to demand their names and business.

"And who are you?" said the first man, who was Despard. "What do you want with us?"

"I am Major Dujardin, and I am officer of the night. I demand your passes."

"You shall have them, major. It seems to me, however, that my name ought to be sufficient."

"And what is your name?"

"Andrew Despard."

"Diable! How came you out on such a night as this? Look you here—you have betrayed me."

"In what manner?"

"Others have the secrets which you have held. I know it, because this very night they have been revealed to me by at least two persons."

"Did they say they had the knowledge from me, Major Dujardin?"

"No."

"They never had their knowledge from me, whoever they may be. And yet, there is some one in Montreal who knows my history: how, I can not tell. Shall we pass on?"

"Not until I see your passes."

"I thought my name a sufficient pass."

"It is not, however."

"Very good. Take us to head-quarters."

"That is unnecessary."

"By no means. I have a little tale to tell the Governor. He will be interested, no doubt. Here is my pass, if it is sufficient."

It was not yet late, and Dujardin looked it over by the light of a lamp in a window near which they stood.

"'Doctor Despard and assistant.' Very well; let your assistant step forward; I must see his face," he said.

"Why do you wish to see his face?"

"That is nothing to you. I tell you I suspect you very grievously, Doctor Despard. Come forward, sir. If there is nothing wrong here, there is no reason why I should not see your face."

"Vraiment," said Wilton, "any thing you choose. But, upon my word, you astonish me."

He came close up to the major, who removed the cloak and peered into his face. Before he had time to utter a cry of surprise, he was seized by the throat and hurled to the ground. A terrible struggle took place, and Dujardin managed to get his mouth free and shout for assistance. There was no help for it now. A dagger gleamed in air, and Mariot Dujardin had seen his last of earth, but that a man ran out of a house near which the struggle took place, and seized the arm of Despard.

"Run for it," cried the spy; "I am taken."

Wilton saw that his friend had now three men upon him, and that a dozen more were hurrying up from different points. There was nothing for it but to run, and attempt his rescue afterward if possible. He darted down a side street, leaving his friend struggling with an overwhelming force of his enemies.

It cut Wilton to the heart to be forced to do this, but he knew that Despard would not misjudge him. Several men pursued the fugitive a short distance, and then gave it up. Despard was overpowered by this time, and was standing, held back by each arm, facing Dujardin.

"Ah-ha!" cried the latter. "So you are a spy? I would have given five of the best years of my life to know this before."

"The minutes of your life would have been numbered, but for these," replied Despard, sternly. "It is well for you that yonder man stopped the dagger. A stout arm, nerved by vengeance, is sure to drive a stiff blade home."

"I have you—I have you! Devil, who will believe your

story now ? Ah, you are the masked man who seized the Governor and Secretary."

Despard was silent. They took him away and plunged him into their strongest cell, where he lay all night, with a guard standing over him, with a bayonet at his breast. When morning came he was led out for trial.

CHAPTER IX.

A STRANGE MEETING.

THEY brought him out, heavily guarded, and set him face to face with the Governor and council. Looking about upon the many faces in the room, Despard could not see one which had any sympathy with him. Every countenance expressed a firm determination. Indeed, he looked for no mercy. It had been a part of his plan to meet death bravely, if by any chance he fell into the hands of the enemy. There was a half-defiant look in his face which surprised them.

"Doctor Andrew Despard," said the Governor, gravely, "you stand here charged with a grave crime. Far be it from me to anticipate your sentence. I hope that your witnesses may be strong enough to bear down the array of proof which can be brought against you. The crime with which you are charged is that of betraying the country which gave you birth, to our enemies. I hope it is untrue."

"Sir," said Despard, promptly, "as for betraying the country which gave me birth, let me say to you what I have never said to a Frenchman before: I am an Englishman."

"An Englishman !"

"Yes. What I have done, I have done. I had an object in it. Go on with the trial, since you assure me of a fair one. I believe you honorable enough to accord me that."

A murmur of surprise and anger ran through the assembly. They had no compassion for him now. An Englishman ! Then he had deceived them all these years.

"Doctor Despard," said the Governor, "you are accused of

being an English spy. What say you to the charge? Guilty
or not guilty?"

"Guilty!" said Despard. "Yes, a thousand times guilty.
I am proud of what I have done. I should go to my grave
in sorrow, and never rest quietly there, if I had not this
thought to sustain me. For years I have labored to do what
I could to break down the power and glory of France in this
section. I am proud in the belief that I have done it well.
The foe is at your gates. Yet a few hours, and this proud
city will be overrun by English troops. I had hoped to see
it and triumph in it. I am only grieved to lose this satisfaction."

"He confesses," said the Governor. "Secretary, make a
minute of his words. You know what your fate will be,
Despard. I wish to learn some things which have always
been shrouded in mystery. Will you answer my questions?"

"With pleasure; you have treated me well," replied Despard.

"In the first place, let me ask who it was took the plan of
our last campaign from the table before me, at the council in
the castle? The light was accidentally overturned, and when
again relighted, the paper was gone."

"*I* took it," said Despard, quietly.

You have heard a snarl run through a cage of wild beasts
when the tamer appears among them. A sound much like
this was heard in the room at this confession. The loss of
that paper had nearly ruined a good campaign.

"You sent it to the English?"

"Yes; Wilton took it to them."

"Who aided this Wilton, known as the Silent Slayer, to
escape?"

"I did," replied Despard. "When we parted, after his escape, I gave him the paper."

"Myself and Secretary were set upon the other night in
the street, and robbed of important papers. One of the men
who seized us was this same Wilton. Who was his companion?"

"It was myself," replied Despard, with a quiet smile.

"You! It is impossible! That man was an uncouth

Englishman, and spoke in the rough, rude way their *creaters* have."

"Nevertheless, it was I," said Despard. "You know nothing of my disguises. I have come to you in more shapes than one. As Doctor Despard I am well known to you, but I have other shapes."

At this moment there was a clamor at the door; the guards scattered right and left, and Conrad broke in. His distorted figure seemed to grow as he stood before them.

"What means all this? Have they harmed you, Andrew?"

"No, good Conrad. Why do you come here? You can do me no good."

"I can at least die by your side," said Conrad, firmly.

"Let me beg you to retire, Conrad. My course is run. I have confessed that I am a spy of the English. My sentence will be death. You must go away."

"Not yet," said Dujardin. "Order the guards to seize this fellow, my chief. He is the friend of Despard, and no doubt privy to his designs."

"His friend, Mariot Dujardin? Yes, and *thy* enemy to the death!"

"Go away, Conrad. If you love me, do not make my last hours bitter by such words as these. You will only do yourself harm. Go!"

"Listen to me," said Conrad. "To all you who stand gaping at me, I here proclaim that I have been the aider and abettor of this man Despard in all his acts against the power and glory of France. Not an act of his have I not been cognizant of. I have carried messages in the dead of night from man to man. I have plotted in secret, all for the downfall of France."

"Seize him!" cried the Governor.

"He has destroyed himself," murmured Despard. "I am fatal to all who love me. It were better that I were in my grave."

But Conrad fell at his feet, and wrapped his long arms about his knees.

"My master," he cried, "we will die together. Conrad Dumont never can hope for a better fate than this. I have lived

by your side, and you shall see me die as bravely as if I had
a better form than this."

The guards laid hands upon him.

"Off, you vile pack!" he shouted. "Off, I say! I am
your prisoner, and shall not attempt to escape. Fools that
you are, do you not see that I came here to die? Why should
I escape when *he* stands there?"

"Nothing now remains," said the Governor, making a signal to the guards to stand back, "but to ask the decision of
the court. Of your guilt there remains no doubt, for both
confess it. Before I ask the decision of this court, let me ask
you, where is the English spy, the Silent Slayer?"

"I know not. Safe from your hands, I hope. Come, your
sentence. Give me your hand, my noble Conrad; we can
die bravely yet. It is something, after all, to know that we
have been true to each other, and to our oaths, this many a
year."

"Silence!" said Dujardin, stooping over from the place
where he stood, and striking the prisoner on the mouth with
the flat of his hand.

Despard had endured much that day—the threats of the
eyes about him, the gallows before him, the sacrifice of Conrad, and the ill-concealed triumph in the face of Dujardin.
But, when he felt the blow, he lifted his manacled hands and
brought them down with resistless force upon the head of the
insulter. Nothing but the thick cap he wore prevented his
skull from being beaten in like an eggshell. As it was, he lay
prostrate, the blood gushing in a gory stream from his mouth
and nose.

"He has killed him," said one of the officers, as he stooped
to raise him.

"Served him right, for striking a prisoner," said another.

"Eh, bien," said D'Aumale, the Secretary, taking snuff to
an alarming extent, "he strikes well. Ah-ha, Monsieur Dujardin!"

"Is he dead?" said the Governor.

"No, your excellency, only stunned."

"Take him out. Gentlemen, you who adjudge these men
guilty of death, raise your right hands."

Every hand was raised, and the Governor stood up.

"You, Doctor Andrew Despard, and you, Conrad Dumont, upon your own confession, are adjudged guilty of death by this council. It remains for me to pass sentence upon you. You will proceed from this place to the prison, and from that prison you will be led out to-morrow at eight o'clock in the morning to the place of execution, and there hanged by the neck till you are dead ; and may the Saints have mercy on your souls."

The stern guard closed in about them and conducted them again to prison. The room in which they were to be confined was a strong one, in the center of the building—a room which, even if the prisoner managed to break, would leave him within the prison still. They heard the heavy bolts and bars fall, and knew that all hope was gone. It was their last day on earth.

Despard lay down upon the hard bed and hid his face. Conrad crouched at his feet, like a faithful dog. It was his nature to give up all for the master he loved, as a servant never loved master before in all his time.

A fearful thing is it to wait in prison for the death which comes upon the morrow !

Despard had nerved himself to meet his fate, and yet it was terrible. He had been more happy since he had the love and sympathy of Marie and her lover. He had even dreamed of a life which, while it could never be truly happy, would be better than his career for the past years. All those hopes were ashes now.

"I should like to see Dujardin once before I die," said Despard. "I should like to have him know what it is which has blocked his way so much since he came to Montreal."

"You can write it," said Conrad.

"I will do it," said he. "He shall know that it is the avenger of Terese who followed him and made his life bitter to him."

The jailer came in, bringing them food. Neither had much appetite. The fellow stood by until they pushed the dishes back, and then took them up to go. Despard looked him in the face.

"Your name is Justin June," said he. "Come here. I wish to speak to you."

"Against orders, messieurs. I must go," replied the keeper.

"Oh, but I have something to tell either to you or the Governor," said Despard. "Do you remember the escape of a prisoner from this very room three years ago? I remember that there was some mystery in the matter, to the authorities. There was none to me. The man who escaped told me who helped him."

"Be quiet, can't you?" muttered the man, turning pale. "Why need you bellow it out so loud?"

"I can prove what I say," said Despard. "Come close to me. Either you must do as much for us as you did for that man, or I will inform on you."

"I have heard before that you were the devil, Conrad, and now I believe it," said the man. "You told your master that."

"Speak to the point, my man. Will you assist us?" replied Despard.

"I will try. I must, I suppose."

"Enough. If I do not hear from you an hour after dark, I will send word to the Governor that I have an important revelation to make."

"I'll come," said June. "Don't be too hard on a man. What will you give?"

"I will make you rich enough to buy the house you have been looking at so long, and to marry little Marianna Lefebre, whom you love so well. Now go. And let me hear from you soon."

The jailer took up his dishes and departed. He soon after left the prison, and at a Jew shop near the river, purchased a rope about ten fathoms in length. This purchase caused considerable playful banter between himself and the shop-keeper as to the use he intended to make of it. As he turned to leave the shop some one touched him on the shoulder. He turned quickly. A lady, closely vailed, stood by his side.

"You are Justin June, the jailer, are you not?" she said.

"The same, madame," he answered.

"Come to the Rue Bartolemy in half an hour. A large house, near the corner of the alley. It has a brown door and heavy shutters," she said.

"I know the place," said the jailer. "Why should I come there?"

"I will make it worth your trouble," said the lady. "You would do well to come."

"Just as you think. I must go at once, if I go at all. I have no time to waste."

"Go on, then. I will be with you soon."

An hour after, the jailer left the large house in the Rue Bartolemy, with a smiling and determined visage. Whatever the reasons for calling him there might have been, it was evident that they accorded with his own views.

He managed to make an errand to the cell of Despard shortly after, and while busy in looking at the fastenings of his fetters, whispered:

"Observe what I drop upon the bed."

It was a small key, exactly like the one he was fitting into the fetters. Despard covered it with his hand and managed to slip it into his pocket.

"Very good," said the jailer. "Now observe that nothing can be done until I give you a signal which you will understand when it comes. By the way, you have a lady working for you."

"*Marie D'Arigny?*"

"No. I know *her* very well. It is a lady who lives in the Rue Bartolemy. She said your life was dearer to her than her own."

"Conrad," said Despard, "am I going mad? What woman is there in all the world, beside Marie, who cares for me? She must be mistaken in her man, Justin."

"No. She gave your name in full. I am to meet her outside the walls to-night and arrange a little plan. Be tranquil. We may do something for you yet."

"If I had a weapon."

"You shall have one. I must leave you now."

When he was gone, a new hope sprung up in the bosoms of the two men. But, Despard could not understand who this lady of the Rue Bartolemy could be. He racked his brain in vain. To be sure, he had befriended many a poor woman by his knowledge of medicine, but this one the jailer described as a "lady." Who *could* it be?

The hours passed in feverish anxiety. It grew dark and the jailer entered, accompanied by an officer, and they looked over the irons of the prisoners together.

"Where is your key?" said the officer.

The jailer took it from a pocket in his blouse and gave it to him. He fitted it into the lock of the fetters, satisfied himself that they were strong, and returned the key to the jailer.

"This is your last visit to-night, is it not?" said the jailer.

"I come again at two in the morning," replied the officer.

"Then the prisoners had better try and get a little rest. They have not much time to waste, and what they have to do to close up their accounts must be done *at once.*"

Despard understood the emphasis put upon the last two words. The two passed out and the jingle of the officer's spurs sounded along the passage. Despard produced the key and unlocked the fetters upon Conrad's hands and feet. The deformed man then did the same kind office for his master. This had hardly been done, when a slight sound in the rear of the room attracted their attention. Looking that way, Despard saw a large stone which formed part of the wall begin to move, and the next moment it swung aside, revealing an opening large enough to admit the body of a man. The face of Justin June appeared at this opening, and he beckoned them silently to come. They had already removed their boots and moved noiselessly over the floor. Conrad passed through the opening first, and was followed by Despard. They found themselves in a sort of alley between two cells. June seized a hand of each, and led them away. Familiar with every inch of the building, in which he had been employed for ten years, he led them on. To the surprise of Despard, he went toward the top of the building, never loosening his hold of their hands, nor speaking a word. They understood the necessity of caution and scarcely breathed. A sense of the danger kept them silent. They knew that guards were posted in every part of the building, and that only the skill and knowledge of the prison possessed by the jailer could carry them safely through the toils. At last they stood upon the roof of the prison. It was one of those flat-topped structures then in vogue, with a parapet

about two feet high. They stood there, and looked out upon
the city. An unusual stir could be noted in the streets, for
that hour of the night. Men were hurrying by in the greatest
dismay, shouting to each other.

"What means this?" said Despard, in a whisper.

"The English," replied the jailer.

"Ha! Are they here?"

"They are coming in force. D'Levi has been beaten back
from Quebec, after beating the enemy in the open field. Ah,
bah! It is all over with us in Canada."

"Thank God," said Despard. "I have waited and watched
for this. That man loves France. Her honor and glory he
has always placed before his own. I can die contented, if
France is beaten."

"You would do better to see about your escape," said the
jailer, angrily.

"You are right. How is it to be done from this point?"

"Easily enough. Here is a rope. Tie it to this chimney."

They fastened it firmly, and drew the knot tight. "Go
down," said Despard, waving his hand.

"You first, my master," replied Conrad; "and when you
reach the ground, wait not for me, but escape for your
life."

It was not a time to dally. Despard dropped over the parapet and slid to the earth. Conrad followed. The jailer remained upon the roof. Some one, wrapped in a cloak, received them below.

"This way," said a low voice.

"What is this?" cried some one at this moment. "They
escape. *Feu*, camarades, *feu!*"

A blaze of light from a dozen muskets illuminated the
scene. Despard saw the person who had received him stag-
ger, and satisfied that he had received some hurt, caught him
up in his arms, and calling to Conrad to follow, darted down a
side street, toward the river, in the way he expected the
English troops. He knew that, by this time, they must have
been pushed far up the island, and he hoped to find some of
their outposts. He was not surprised when a deep voice
cried in English:

"*Who goes there?*"

"A friend," cried Despard. "If you are Englishmen, give me aid."

"Gracious heaven!" cried the challenger, "*it is Despard!*"

"*Wilton!*"

"The very man. Old friend, this cheers my heart. I never thought to look upon your face again."

"No time for words. I am pursued. Have you a boat?"

"Yes; I was coming to your aid. I meant to bring you off, or leave my scalp in Montreal. Stand close, boys. Here they come. Give them a taste of your rifles. That will sicken them."

A sharp clicking sound succeeded the order as the men cocked their rifles. They formed a part of that famous band of rangers who did such distinguished service in the Canadian wars. Their green uniforms and jaunty caps told that to Despard, who knew the corps. But their number was small—a few picked scouts who could be trusted in such a service as this, and who had been smuggled out of camp one at a time to escape the prying eyes of Putnam, Lewis and Warren, who would not have allowed some of their best men to go on so desperate an enterprise.

A motley group of soldiers, Indians, and Canadian partisans came on in pursuit. Those deadly rifles were lifted, and a close fire poured in the crowded mass. They swayed back with yells of terror, having got into a hornet's nest without knowing it.

"Into the boat," cried Wilton. "I wonder how they liked that? Why, what have you here, Despard?"

"A young fellow who helped me to escape. I'm afraid he is hurt."

"Not much," said a feeble voice. "It is in my shoulder."

"I say," said Jake Dowdle, a famous scout of the Champlain region, who had come out with the party, "seems to me that's a gal's voice."

At this moment a rocket was sent up on the river below them.

By the momentary glare, Despard caught a glimpse of the face which lay in the hollow of his arm. He uttered a cry, half in joy, half in sorrow, and tore the cloak away.

"Terese! I call you by that name by which I knew you in

those happy days in Normandy. Speak, and tell me that I do not dream, and a life of agony is atoned for, in the bliss of this moment."

"Hold me close to your heart, Charles. We will never be parted again."

It was a strange meeting. In the darkness, upon the flowing river, he held the woman he so tenderly loved even when he thought she lay in her grave, close to his beating heart. The sorrow of the past was all forgotten then. The men in the boat kept silence. Though but rough border men, they recognized in this the work of the Deity we all adore.

"Oars," said Wilton. "We have trouble ahead. Keep your rifles handy. I don't like those rockets. If the Governor only could get a chance to hang me to-night, I think he would be content to give up the city to-morrow. Ha; there is a canoe. Into her!"

They bent to their oars. There was a crash, and the stout bateau glided over the demolished canoe, leaving the occupants struggling in the river. A wild shout from the rangers attested their triumph. It was of short duration, however. The stream below them seemed to be alive with lights, and they knew that their retreat was cut off below. It was hard. Not half-a-mile now intervened between them and the troops of the English, who were camped upon the island, under the lead of Colonel Haviland.

The spy had known that they were near at hand, but had not thought them so near as this. All the tumult and disarray he had seen that night were caused by the entrance into the city of M. de Bourlemaque, at the head of the forces which had been forced back by the coming of Murray and Lord Rollo. On the other hand, Haviland had forced De Bourgainville into the city from the other side; and sixteen thousand men now lay camped about the city walls. Montreal was doomed.

Nearly frantic with rage at the great loss which was coming upon France, the leading men in Montreal cared more for the taking of these spies than they would have done under any other circumstances. The river was lined with troops. The woods were full of Indians. In this extremity, they adopted a plan which, for boldness, has few parallels in history.

They turned back and reëntered the city.

In the confusion then existing, and in the darkness, it was a comparatively easy thing to reach Anselmo's house. Conrad led them, and knowing the house well, he undertook to find the key. This done, the men, some ten ... number, entered the house. No light was needed ; Despard guided them to the secret place in the wall and sent them in.

"How is this?" said one of the men ; "neatest hiding place I ever saw. This is *rather* cute : ten of old Put and Rogers' best scouts cooped up in the city ! Suppose our men get licked, what a nice box we would be in, to be sure !"

"Rather," said Jake Dowdle. "You'd like it, I s'pose, you durned fool."

"The house has a double wall, as you see," said Despard. "That is some of Conrad's work. He is a mason by trade, and delights in building queer hiding-places."

"I thought Conrad never cared for any man but you," said Wilton.

"He will do any thing for Anselmo which he will do for me," said Despard. "Do not keep me here ; I must go to Terese ; she is hurt. Oh, my God, what if she should die now !"

"I trust not, Despard," said Wilton. "I hope you have before you many happy years ; you deserve them, if any man does."

"I don't know ; I have a strange foreboding that all is not over yet. Let me go now."

He went back to the rooms above ; Terese was still lying upon the couch where he had placed her, with Conrad bending over her. The faithful fellow was nearly mad with joy ; the mistress he had loved so dearly had come back to him. Despard dressed the wound, which was slight, and then placing her head upon his breast, drew from her the story of her life. He found that she had spent eight years in a convent, without taking the vail. At the end of that time, a man who had been in Montreal told in her hearing that he had seen a man in Canada, who called himself Despard, who was her lost lover. She left the convent and came to Canada. Here she spent a year in searching for Despard, and she found him engaged in the execution of a vow. She had a talent for painting. The pictures which Dujardin had seen upon the wall were painted by her, and the effect was produced by curtains, which made the pictures seem to be thrown upon the wall itself. She had met Despard but once, and that was on the night when he stopped her in the street.

The night was short to them; the daylight came, and found them still seated there, talking of the strange events which had befallen them since the time when Despard fled, with the brand of felon on him, and Terese was thought to have found a grave under the waters of the Seine. The ten years which had passed had not changed the heart of either, and they loved more ardently now than when they roamed, hand in hand, through the verdant groves of Normandy.

Forgetful of every thing, they did not see the face which was peering in at the window. It was that of Langlier, the man who had seen Wilton on the occasion of his first visit to the house of Anselmo! He remained a moment in doubt, and then stole silently away.

It was nearly noon before any thing was done. Despard sent some food and wine to the men imprisoned in the wall, and remained himself to attend to the comfort of Terese. He did not notice the broken blind, or, with his keen head, he would have suspected something. Conrad determined to risk a visit to Marie. He slipped over the garden wall, and entered the house through the kitchen. Here he found Annette, who told him that articles of capitulation were being drawn up, and that the party had only to remain quiet for a few hours, and all would be well. He hurried back after telling Annette what to say to Marie, and went to the room where his master was. To his surprise, it was full of armed men, under the leadership of Dujardin, who seemed to hunt Despard with demoniac hate. The latter, armed only with a sword, was standing before the lady, when Conrad dashed in and stood at his side. Despard was speaking.

"You do not know me, Mariot Dujardin; you have never known me. I will tell you my name. Look at her face: do you know her?"

"Terese D'Arcy! Then she is not dead, and I have been

frightened by your ingenious clap-trap. Very good; and who are you?"

"I am one who has laid you on your back in fair battle—Charles Armand! Do you remember the name?"

A cry of triumph broke from the lips of Dujardin.

"And are you indeed that escaped murderer? How fortune plays into my hands! As I live, this is the best hour of my life. The city is surrendered, the English are already pouring in; but they will not be in time to save your life. Down with them, boys! You shall die before her eyes."

Conrad's eyes brightened when the villain said the city was surrendered. Springing to the wall, he touched a spring, and a huge panel slid down. Out of the opening came the green-coated rangers, and drove back the motley group in the room. But, they were not quick enough to prevent the strife between Despard and Dujardin. All the wrongs which had been heaped upon him, all the bitterness of ten years, gave strength to the spy's arm and keenness to his eye.

When the French surged back before the rifles of the rangers, Dujardin lay face upward on the floor, and Despard stood above him, looking fixedly into the evil eyes, upon which a film was fast coming. The feud of years had been atoned for at length. Despard extended his hand and said:

"There lies my deadly enemy. Gentlemen, from this day forget that I have been called Despard, the spy. I am Charles Armand, whom he hunted, almost unto death. Frenchmen, I was accused of murder. Speak before you die, Mariot: did I kill that man in France?"

"No," said Dujardin; "I did it. Farewell, friends and foes. I die as I lived, the friend of France, the enemy of England. But my pride is broken, since Wilton and Terese are here to see my fall. Jesu Maria—pardon—my sins."

And, kissing the cross of his sword, he fell back and expired. The French soldiery slunk away, for the hearty English shouts which sounded in the street apprised them of the entrance of the foe. For, on that day, the 8th of September, 1760, the Marquis Vaudreuil signed the capitulation of the city and the whole province of Canada, which passed forever from Canadian rule.

The story draws to a close. Charles Armand, Despard no longer, by the aid of the great wealth which was his, and which he had converted into jewels before his condemnation in France, had been enabled to perform well his work in Montreal. It had come to a happy fruition. In a few days there was a double wedding at the cathedral. The principal officers of the provincial portion of the army attended, and many of the regulars, to attest the high regard in which they held the whilom spies, Despard and Wilton.

Two more beautiful brides had never stepped over the marble floors.

The party returned to Anselmo's house, where the marriage-feast was given. In the midst of the revelry, Despard excused himself for a moment. Shortly after, Anselmo entered, and took Despard's place by the side of Terese. Some of the invited guests looked a little startled, but Anselmo rose and was about to speak, when Terese rose also, and giving the white hair a sudden tug, it dropped to the floor, and Despard stood revealed! Most of those present knew the story of Anselmo, and a shout was raised which made the rafters of the old house tremble.

"Friends," said Charles Armand, " Despard's work is done; Anselmo goes to his grave; but Charles Armand thanks you from his heart and welcomes you to his roof."

They remained in Canada. Conrad continued with the master he loved, until death called him home. Wilton and his beautiful wife went to New York, and settled near Albany. Once in two years they made a journey to Montreal, and in the intervening year received the Armands at their own home. The friendship of the families became historical, in the two provinces.

THE END.

DIME DIALOGUES, No. 1.

Meeting of the Muses; or the Crowning of Florence Nightingale. For nine young ladies.
Baiting a Live Englishman. For three boys.
Tasso's Coronation. For male and female.
Fashion. For two ladies.
The Rehearsal. For six boys.
Which will you Choose? For two boys.
The Queen of May. For two little girls.
The Tea-Party. For four ladies.
Three Scenes in the Wedded Life of Mr. Bradley. For male and female.
Mrs. Sniffles' Confession. For male and female.

The Mission of the Spirits. For five young ladies
Hobnobbing. For five speakers.
The Secret of Success. For three male speakers.
Young America. For three male and two females.
The Destiny of the Empress Josephine. For four females and one male.
The Folly of the Duel. For three male speakers.
Dog-matism. For three male speakers.
The Year's reckoning. For twelve females and one male.
The Village with one Gentleman. For eight females and one male.

DIME DIALOGUES, No. 2.

The Genius of Liberty. For two males and one female.
Cinderella; or, the Little Glass Slipper.
The Society for Doing Good and Saying Bad. For several characters.
The Golden Rule. For two males and two females.
The Gift of the Fairy Queen. For several females.
Taken in and Done For. For two characters.
The Country Aunt's Visit to the City. For several characters.
The Two Romans. For two males.
Trying the Characters. For three males.
The Happy Family. For several "animals."

The Rainbow. For several characters.
How to Write "Popular" Stories. For two males.
The New and the Old. For two males.
A Sensation at Last. For two males.
The Greenhorn. For two males.
The Three Men of Science. For four males.
The Old Lady's Will. For four males.
The Little Philosophers. For two little girls.
How to Find an Heir. For five males.
The Virtues. For six young ladies.
The Public Meeting. For five males and one female.
The English Traveler. For two males.

DIME DIALOGUES, No. 3.

The May Queen. Musical and Floral Drama, as performed at the Convent of Notre Dame, Cincinnati. For an entire school.
The Dress Reform Convention. For ten females.
Keeping Bad Company. A Farce. For five males.
Courtship under Difficulties. A Commedietta. For two males and one female.
National Representatives. A Burlesque. For four males.
Escaping the Draft. A Commedietta For numerous male characters.

The Genteel Cook. A Humorous Colloquy. For two males.
Masterpiece. A Dramatic Charade. For two males and two females.
The Two Romans. A Colloquy on costume. For two males.
The Same. Second Scene. For two males.
Showing the White Feather. A Farce. For four males and one female.
The Battle Call. A Recitative. For one male

DIME DIALOGUES, No. 4.

The Frost King. A Scenic Drama. For ten or more persons.
Starting in Life. A Petite Farce. For three males and two females.
Faith, Hope, and Charity. A Colloquy in verse. For three little girls.
Darby and Joan. A Minor Drama. For two males and one female.
The May. A Floral Fancy. For six little girls.
The Enchanted Princess. A Burlesque Divertissement. For two males and several females.
Honor to whom Honor is Due. A Colloquy. For seven males and one female.
Phrenology. A Discussion. For twenty males.

The Stubbletown Volunteer. A Farce. For three males and one female.
A Scene from "Paul Pry." For four males.
The Charms. A Parlor Drama. For three males and one female.
Bee, Clock, and Broom. A Rhymed Fancy. For three little girls.
The Right Way. A Colloquy. For two boys.
What the Ledger Says. A "Negro" Burlesque. For two males.
The Crimes of Dress. A Colloquy. For two boys.
The Reward of Benevolence. A minor Drama. For four males.
The Letter. For two males.

DIME DIALOGUES, No. 5.

The Three Guesses. A Fairy Extravaganza. For school or parlor.
Sentiment. A "Three Persons" Farce.
Behind the Curtain. A Domestic Commedietta. For several characters, male and female.
The Eta Pi Society. A Juvenile Farce. For five boys and a teacher.
Examination Day at Madame Savante's. A droll Episode. For several female characters.
Trading in "Traps." A serio-comic passage. For several male characters.
The School-Boys' Tribunal. A Dramatic Episode. For ten or more boys.
What comes of a Loose Tongue. A Domestic

Interlude. For several male and female characters.
How not to Get an Answer. A Colloquy. For two females.
Putting on Airs. A Colloquy. For two males.
The Straight Mark. A School Experience. For several boys.
Two Ideas of Life. A Colloquy. For ten girls.
Extract from Marino Faliero.
Ma-try-money. An Acting Charade. A Parlor Drama.
The Six Virtues. For Six young ladies.
Fashionable Requirements. For three girls.
A Bevy of I's (eyes.) For eight, or less, little girls

DIME DIALOGUES, No. 6.

The Way they Kept a Secret. For seven females and one male.
The Poet under Difficulties. For five males.
William Tell. For a whole school.
Woman's Rights. For seven females and two males.
All is not Gold that Glitters. For three females and one male.
The Generous Jew. For six males.

Shopping. For three females and one male.
The Two Counsellors. For three males.
The Votaries of Folly. For a number of females.
Aunt Betsy's Beaux. For four females and two males.
The Libel Suit. For two females and one male.
Santa Claus. For a number of boys.
Christmas Fairies. For several little girls.
The Three Rings. For two males.

DIME DIALOGUES, No. 7.

The Two Beggars. A Minor Drama. For fourteen females.
The Earth-Child in Fairy-Land. A Fairy-Land Court Scene. For numerous girls.
Twenty Years Hence. A Serio-Comical Passage. For two females and one male.
The Way to Windham. A Colloquy. For two males.
Woman. A Poetic Passage at Words. For two boys.
The 'Ologies. A Colloquy. For two males.
How to Get Rid of a Bore. A School Drama. For several boys.
Boarding-School Accomplishments. A School Drama. For two males and two females.
A Plea for the Pledge. A Colloquy. For two persons.
Dram-Drinking. A Colloquy. For two females.
A Colloquy. For two females.
A Two Painters. A Burlesque. For numerous males.

Two Views of Life. A Colloquy. For two males.
The Rights of Music. A Colloquy and something else. For two females.
A Hopeless Case. A Query in Verse. For two girls.
The Would-be School-Teacher. A School Examiner's Experience. For two males.
Come to Life too Soon. A Humorous Passage. For three males.
Eight O'clock. A Little Girls' Colloquy. For two little children.
True Dignity. A Colloquy. For two boys.
Grief too Expensive. A Colloquy. For two males.
Hamlet and the Ghost. A Burlesque. For two persons.
Little Red Riding Hood. A Nursery Lesson. For two females.
A New Application of an Old Rule. A Colloquial Passage. For two boys and one girl.
Colored Cousins. A "Colored" Colloquy. For two males.

A choice collection of original School and Parlor Colloquies, Dramas, Commediettas, Burlesques, Farces, etc., adapted for any stage, platform or room, each book containing one hundred 12mo. pages. For sale by all newsdealers; or sent, post-paid, to any address, on receipt of price, ten cents each.

BEADLE AND COMPANY, Publishers, 98 William street, N. Y.

Lightning Source UK Ltd.
Milton Keynes UK
UKOW022036010513

210073UK00010B/575/P